# DECONSTRUCTING
# THEODICY

# Deconstructing Theodicy

Why Job Has Nothing to Say
to the Puzzled Suffering

## David B. Burrell, CSC
## with A. H. Johns

**BrazosPress**

*a division of Baker Publishing Group*
Grand Rapids, Michigan

Published by Brazos Press
a division of Baker Publishing Group
P.O. Box 6287, Grand Rapids, MI 49516-6287
www.brazospress.com

Printed in the United States of America

Library of Congress Cataloging-in-Publication Data
Burrell, David B.
    Deconstructing theodicy : why Job has nothing to say to the puzzled suffer-
ing / David B. Burrell.
        p.   cm.
    Includes bibliographical references and index.
    ISBN 978-1-58743-222-4 (pbk.)
    1. Bible. O. T. Job—Criticism, interpretation, etc. 2. Theodicy—Biblical
teaching. I. Title.
BS1415.52.B87  2008
223'.106—dc22                                                    2007029475

To
† Frère Marcel Dubois, OP
Jerusalem
and
Frère Jean-Jacques Perennès, OP
and the Dominican Community
Cairo

# CONTENTS

# PREFACE

NE HAS ONLY to consult a blockbuster commentary like that of David Clines to be humbled in the face of even attempting a "theological reflection" of this "strange and wonderful book" (Maimonides). Yet the modifier *theological* allows us to borrow freely from those whose lens is more philological and literary, as we shall indeed do, while allowing us to focus on the fruitfulness of this key scriptural work for the prosecution of philosophical theology today. My own enthusiasm to take up this task stemmed from an intuition that clarifying the role of this book in the Hebrew scriptures could also affect much of what passes for *theodicy* in contemporary philosophy of religion. The book of Job inserts itself into the Hebrew canon as a trenchant critique of a unilateral application of the Deuteronomic formula for the covenant of God with Israel: that observance of the terms of the covenant will be rewarded and deviation punished. Might it also be that any attempt to *explain* the ways of God to human beings will face a similar critique? I shall argue that the very structure of the book of Job may be extended in such a way and so offers a salient critique of classical and contemporary theodicies.

Translations of the book abound; I have utilized (with the translator's permission) one completed at the Tantur Ecumenical Institute (Jerusalem) in the midst of the first Gulf War (1990) by a scholar from Slovenia, Dr. Juij Bizjak, currently serving as a Catholic bishop in that country. While the book of Job is replete with subtle literary features, as astute commentators will observe, we shall focus primarily on the difference in speech acts between the protagonist and his interlocutors, for that very difference seems to herald the book's significance for inquirers in philosophical theology. Moreover, beyond customary biblical commentaries, monographs celebrating the book's teaching abound as well. I will only mention three that have affected me: those of Gustavo Gutiérrez (1987), John Wilcox (1989), and Bruce Zuckerman (1991).

The book of Job is replete with poetic repetition, which suggests that line-by-line commentary would distract from the impact of such repetition. So this reflection contents itself with employing strategic citations to identify thematic patterns in the work itself, allowing the poetic repetition to do its work unimpeded (Pickstock 1998). After following those patterns through the text, we will be able to call upon them to illuminate the central questions of our inquiry, as well as use them to address other approaches to these issues as well.

The dedication expresses a longstanding gratitude to my Dominican mentor in Jerusalem, Marcel Dubois (1920–2007), as well as one which I share with A. H. Johns for the intellectual and personal hospitality of the Dominican community in Cairo, in the person of its sometime prior, Jean-Jacques Perrenès. The personal and intellectual environment of Tantur Ecumenical Institute in Jerusalem made this work possible through its rector, Michael McGarry, CSP, with Mrs. Vivi Siniora, the house matron of seventeen years, and now vice-rector, Bridget Tighe, FMDM, who together create a home for students and scholars of all ages and nationalities, in a thirty-five acre oasis at a checkpoint, so the realities of the Holy Land are never far away. Eleanor Stump provided the original impetus to venture on this journey, through a shared reading of Aquinas's commentary some years ago, and more recently sharing with me her Gifford manuscript, while Edward Greenstein offered an unexpected corroboration of these directions from a scripture scholar, in his "Truth or Theodicy? Speaking Truth to Power in the Book of Job," *Princeton Seminary Bulletin* 27 (2006) 238–58.

Finally, my continuing thanks to those who commissioned this study, Russell Reno and Robert Jenson, then to Rodney Clapp, who selected it for publication, and Rebecca Cooper, who shepherded it along its way at Brazos, in whose list of distinguished authors I am privileged to share.

# 1

# Introducing
# the Strategies
# of This Reflection

I
T MAY HARDLY seem ironic to many that the plight of
Job should have generated scores of "theodicies." Yet it
will be the contention of this study that the book that
took his name is expressly intended to deconstruct those very
theories that many have felt it necessary to concoct in response
to the plight of Job. Such theories suggest how Wittgenstein
might have felt to find modes of philosophizing he deplored
resurging; so how better respect his memory than to employ
a "theological reflection" to deconstruct philosophic preten-
sions? And what could be more pretentious than attempting to
"justify the ways of God to us," as the venture of theodicy has
classically been described? (The term *theodicy* was introduced
by Leibniz in his *Concernant la bonté de Dieu, la liberté de*

*l'homme, et l'origine du mal* [1710], in response to Pierre Bayle's contention that the very presence of evil in the created world constituted a prima facie argument against the existence of a good creator-God.) While the intent of that formula may well have been ironic in Milton's employ, many philosophers long after Socrates have lost an ear for irony. Yet while modernity sought to supplant theological reflection with philosophical clarification, or narratives with theories, one of the features that renders postmodernity "post-" is its tendency toward nonreduction, toward juxtaposing diverse modes of discourse in the interest of understanding what each seeks to expound. Admittedly, this is a benign postmodernity, akin to that of John Henry Newman, Bernard Lonergan, or even (at times) John Paul II; and Job will remind us that what makes theirs benign is precisely its grounding in scripture. Yet scriptures can leave ambiguous legacies, as Jews and Christians (with Muslims) know so well, and it is one such legacy in the Hebrew scriptures that the book of Job seeks explicitly to correct. Moreover, we shall see how it accomplishes that by deconstructing theories designed to do an even better job of disambiguating the scriptures than scripture itself attempted in the book of Job.

It is true that the very narrative framing of Job's story—a divinity bargaining with its alter-ego, Satan—sets up a quasi-philosophical problematic, inviting modernist reduction. Yet placing that framing conceit in the larger scriptural context that the entire book presumes, while it busies itself criticizing a narrow appropriation of it, will allow us to appreciate how God-soaked that context is. So a "theological reflection" will be pressed to an enhanced philosophical awareness as it becomes alert to the ways "theology" can also compromise the faith-context it seeks to articulate. Yet *reflection* it must be, for the book itself emanates a ray of hope, finding its way through multiple baffle-plates like the sun at its winter solstice illuminating the headstone at Newgrange. The role that the book of Job plays in the Hebrew scriptures (to correct misapprehensions endemic to those same scriptures) will guide my effort to delineate the steps that the book provides for deconstructing modernist "theories of theodicy." We will also see how medieval philosophical theologians in the Abrahamic tradition can help us utilize the book itself to expose its purported progeny. Attending closely to its structure should unveil the revealing God, and so provide us with the intellectual strategies needed to show how the theodicies emerging in its wake can often obscure that very revelation. Although at best parallel to our main thesis, offering a contemporary commentary on Job's Qur'anic counterpart, Ayyub, may throw additional light on the impact of this biblical character.

## Structure of the reflection

While an initial reading of the story which frames the book of Job suggests a classical theodicy of divine testing and of reward and punishment, we shall later see (with the help of real friends) just how misguided a reading that is. For now, it will suffice to note how the drama's unfolding belies such a reading, notably in the counterpoint between each of Job's friends and Job himself. For while they each address arguments to Job, his riposte to their arguments is addressed not to them but to the overwhelming presence of the God of Israel, to inaugurate an implicit dialogue vindicated by that same God who ends by announcing his preference for Job above all of them. Indeed, they incur the wrath of that God for attempting vigorously to take God's side! Yet since this is the very One who has taken such care to reveal his ways to a particular people (to whom Job does not belong), one cannot escape concluding that the entire dramatic exchange—between Job and his interlocutors and even more between Job and the God of Israel—must be directed against a recurrent misappropriation of that revelation on the part of the people entrusted with it. So it must be that the book's primary role in the Hebrew canon will be to correct that characteristic misapprehension of the revelation displayed by Job's friends, as their "explanation" of his plight turns on reading the covenant as a set of simple transactions. That is, good things are in store for all who abide by the Torah, while affliction attends anyone who does not, so instructing us to use the fact that Job is afflicted to infer that he must have transgressed God's commands.

In fact, from the way his friends have appropriated the covenant, wrongdoing is at once a necessary and a sufficient condition for affliction as a form of punishment, much as a felicitous life is inherently linked to observance of the right way. Yet it is telling that Job himself seems not to have internalized the simple scheme that his friends both presume and represent, the terms of which seem to be set by the framing story. (Could *that* be why the Creator presents him to Satan as truly just?) Yet the double bind into which they try to press Job is anything but ironic: admit your wrongdoing and repent! For in the terms of the book such an admission would constitute a self-serving prevarication, not unlike those "confessions" elicited by Soviet show-trials. Indeed, Herbert Fingarette has identified this legal dilemma as the authentic dramatic frame of the book: Job could release himself from the bind that his friends create only by perjuring himself (Fingarette 1978). So the dramatic context is an explicitly legal one, as Job himself will express in contending with the God of Israel. Yet Job's conduct of his own defense will also serve to deconstruct that legal context, to culminate in an encounter with that One whom the Hebrew scriptures credit with establishing the context itself. More directly, if the God in question is pictured (however implicitly) as judge, we find Job far less interested in what any judge may think of his defense in the face of his prosecuting friends than he is in appealing directly to the creator-judge himself: "Only grant two things to me, then I will not hide myself from your face: withdraw your hand from me, and do not let dread of you terrify me. Then call, and I will answer; or let me speak, and you reply to me" (13:20–22). Rather than treat the Creator as a judge who must adjudicate by the rules, Job appeals directly to the Creator as the One who sets the very rules under which Job has been told he must consider his affliction as punishment, thereby turning this One into an interlocutor. Moreover, the legal frame gives Job no other choice, for to accept the rules as detailed by his friends would demand that he perjure himself, expressly engaging in the very wrongdoing that he has so far consciously avoided.

Yet forced options do not generate drama of themselves. What distinguishes Job (and wins him divine accolades in the end) will also reveal the corrective operative in the book itself. By addressing himself to the author of the covenant, rather than debating its terms with those purportedly expert in it, Job has grasped what his (ostensibly Israelite) friends missed. The covenant itself is a gift bestowed personally by God on this people, thereby establishing a path by which they could come to realize that they are God's own people. By eluding the legal trap, Job shows his respect for the legal context into which his friends have led him, while proceeding to subvert that context by recognizing what the others fail to note. The ostensible judge is in fact the very One who originally gifted Israel with the covenant, and so will only be shown proper gratitude by a direct address. For in the measure that the covenant is gift, it must be intended to lead those to whom it is given to the giver, rather than serve as an opaque veil between donor and recipient. Of all the protagonists, it is the one who is afflicted, yet not himself an Israelite, who exercises his dignity before the giver of the Torah by speaking directly to him. And even more pointedly, he is speaking to the very One who he acknowledges to be the agent of his affliction! Yet in doing so, Job also bests the trickster figure in the framing story, who so astutely articulated the weakness endemic to the "theology" that framing story presumes (and which his friends will repeat ad nauseam): in effect, if you (God) always reward those who obey you, you will never be able to know why they are doing it.

So let us now turn to the book itself, to see whether it can offer us a way through the dilemmas noted. We shall focus first on its structure rather than on discrete assertions, to see how that structure addresses misapprehensions commonly found among those purportedly formed by the covenant, thereby inserting this book into the enveloping context of the Hebrew scriptures so as to determine the role it plays in that canon. Moreover, this approach is demanded by the poetic composition of the work itself, trading as it does on repetition to reiterate its point. In fact, there are very few "arguments" in this book, though (as we hope to show) the structure itself supplies a powerful argument against the efficacy of *argument* in this domain. So it would be pointless, and betray its very poetic character, to attempt line-by-line commentary, though we shall do as much of that as seems demanded. But we shall then put those interpretative findings to work, in distinct chapters, to show how the book can be read as an adroit deconstruction of the very enterprise of theodicy itself, precisely by operating in a performative rather than a propositional key. In this way, we hope to address two issues at once: an abiding puzzlement on the part of those wedded to theodicy, querying how anyone suffering from affliction could possibly profit from overhearing Job's ranting and raving; and on the other hand, to show those disillusioned with various attempts at theodicy how his rant and rave offers a performative alternative to any attempt to "explain" affliction. A purportedly "theological reflection" must show how "philosophy" can be put to therapeutic use by removing theological obfuscation.

Furthermore, the reflection mode hopes to display how scripture can assist in that role, thereby showing itself to be a revelation by purifying the very tools we also need to elucidate it. As an interfaith bonus, we adapt a recent article by A. H. Johns on Job in the Qur'an, to illustrate by contrast the distinctive features of the biblical text (ch. 5). Then the classical commentary mode will be followed by a comparative exposition of four highly philosophical medieval "theological commentaries" (ch. 6), leading us to the explicitly philosophical milieu where theodicy has currently lodged itself (ch. 7). By that time we will have been equipped to assess Job's contribution to theodicy by contrasting two quite different semantic structures: those involved in explaining something to anyone, and those implicit in directly addressing another (ch. 8).

# 2

# THE STRUCTURE
# OF THE BOOK WITH ITS
# FRAMING STORY

J URIJ BIZJAK, THE Slovenian translator whose text helped to shape this reflection, lays out the Hebrew text perspicuously as follows:[1]

### Prologue: 1–2

| First round | | Second round | | Third round | |
|---|---|---|---|---|---|
| Job: | 3 | Job: | 12–14 | Job: | 21 |
| Eliphaz: | 4–5 | Eliphaz: | 15 | Eliphaz: | 22 |
| Job: | 6–7 | Job: | 16–17 | Job: | 23–24 |
| Bildad: | 8 | Bildad: | 18 | Bildad: | 25 |
| Job: | 9–10 | Job: | 19 | Job: | 26–31 |
| Zopar: | 11 | Zophar: | 20 | | |

1. Jurij Bizjak, *A Key to Job: Translation, Interpretation and Structure of the Book of Job* (Jerusalem: Tantur, 1991). Address of translator: Juri Bizak, Trg Brolo 11, 6000 Koper, Slovenia [jurij.bizjak@rkc.si].

| Denouement | |
| --- | --- |
| Elihu: | 32–37 |
| Lord: | 38–40:2 |
| Job: | 40:3–5 |
| Lord: | 40:6–41:26 |
| Job: | 42:1–6 |
| Epilogue: 42:7–17 | |

## Prologue

The framing story introduces "a man in the land of Uz, whose name was Job" (1:1). Archetypally, "that man was blameless and upright, one who feared God and turned away from evil" (1:2) and (as a result?) was fabulously wealthy, in progeny— seven sons and three daughters—in livestock—thousands of sheep, camel, oxen, donkeys—and with "very many servants; so that this man was the greatest of all the people of the east" (1:3). While his sons and daughters feasted on this abundance, Job himself "would rise early in the morning and offer burnt offerings according to the number of them all; for Job said, 'It may be that my children have sinned, and cursed God in their hearts.' This is what Job always did" (1:5). Here appears a man blessed in all ways, yet apparently free of the ordinary human propensity to regard blessings as his possessions; in fact, everything about him is archetypal, so we are hardly surprised when this fairytale beginning suddenly switches from earth to a heavenly setting where "one day the heavenly beings came to present themselves before the Lord, and Satan also came among them" (1:6).

The point of the setup emerges: the poet will utilize the trickster figure, Satan, to precipitate a test for the one whom the Lord lauds as "my servant Job: there is none like him on the earth, a blameless and upright man who fears God and turns away from evil" (1:8). Indeed, Satan's challenge to the Lord unveils a classic dilemma for any religious system that announces reward and punishment: "Does Job fear God for nothing? Have you not put a fence around him and his house and all that he has . . . ? . . . But stretch out your hand now, and touch all that he has, and he will curse you to your face" (1:9–11). What will happen to that touted "fear of the Lord" when it fails to work to one's own advantage? (Teresa of Avila confronts this dilemma for Christians [Williams 1991, 137–38], as does Rab'ia for early Islam [Smith 1994, 121–28].) Surprisingly enough, the Lord empowers Satan: "all that he has is in your power; only do not stretch out your hand against him" (1:12). Yet in the wake of the sudden loss of all of his children, as well as livestock—donkeys, sheep, camels, along with all of his servants—to a lightning Sabean raid, Job does not break (as Satan predicted he would) but utters his encomium: "Naked I came from my mother's womb, and naked I shall return there; the Lord gave, and the Lord has taken away; blessed be the name of the Lord" (1:21). The author comments, "In all this Job did not sin or charge God with wrongdoing" (1:22). So far, so good, it may seem. Yet the test has barely begun, though the theological terms of the setup have been announced: this God has no compunction about testing his servants, especially those who show themselves faithful. And while Job does not belong to that people whom the Lord of heaven and earth has covenanted as his own, there is no doubt that this is that same God, for he did not hesitate to test his friend Abraham in a heartless way: sacrifice to me your only son who embodies the covenant I have made with you in perpetuity.

Indeed, Satan urges him on to a yet more stringent test when the Lord repeats his earlier formula of praise for Job, this time with greater reason: "Have you considered my servant Job? There is none like him on the earth, a blameless and upright man who fears God and turns away from evil. He still persists in his integrity, although you incited me against him, to destroy him for no reason" (2:3). But of course "the Lord" (1:6) did not destroy Job himself, which leaves Satan the opening: "Skin for skin! All that people have they will give to save their lives. But stretch out your hand now and touch his flesh and bone, and he will curse you to your face." The Lord responds by extending Satan's reach to Job's person: "Very well, he is in your power; only spare his life" (2:4–6). The intricate dance of attribution of agency is intentionally confusing here I suggest, as is the role of the trickster figure: God gives Satan power over him yet goes on to assume responsibility for the results: "you incited me against him" (2:3). Whoever or whatever else may be involved in effecting or facilitating the events that bring harm to us, ultimate responsibility has to lie with the Creator of heaven and earth. That must be understood in the way it is simply presumed in the framing story, so it would be silly for us to try to trace lines of responsibility any more explicitly, since trickster figures always outwit our reasoning capacities. So attempting to use our developed sense of right and wrong to assign blame can only be distracting when dealing with "the Lord," (2:1) for whom inflicting harm may in reality amount to a "test." Better try to understand what this "testing" business is about, which Job's own response will lead us to discover. And here too the quasi-mythic portrait of Job will help us elude the "blame game," since God's "test" cannot be construed as deserved, just as Job's neat insulation from God's own "stiff-necked" people will help the author correct the misapprehensions that very people has developed of their God.

Satan appeals to God to intensify the test by reminding the Creator of our instinct for self-preservation: how will Job respond to personal bodily affliction? With this question, which none of us should feel prepared to answer, we are subtly moved from fairytale to drama. Yet Job is obscurely aware from the outset that he is being tested, so we shall watch him come to realize that it is hardly a test anyone can hope to "pass," with the protagonists so unevenly balanced. Job proceeds to transmute affliction into a demand to know why he is being so tested, quickly realizing that that question cannot be answered either. Yet if it is not possible for one to pass this test, what is its point? The dramatic dialogue, with its successive interlocutors and notable primary protagonist, the Lord, addresses that question. His bodily suffering will elicit "compassionate friends," a role that Job's wife cannot bring herself to fulfill: "Do you still persist in your integrity? Curse God, and die" (2:9). As Socrates invited his companions to usher Xanthippe from his death chamber, Job's spouse apparently removes herself in the wake of a stern rebuke, followed by a second encomium guaranteed to further aggravate her: "You speak as any foolish woman would speak. Shall we receive the good at the hand of God, and not receive the bad" (2:10)? So the coterie will consist of four men in the hovering presence of the Lord. Like Plato's friend Crito, Job's friends initially meant well: upon hearing "of all these troubles that had come upon him, each of them set out from his home—Eliphaz the Temanite, Bildad the Shuhite, and Zophar the Naamathite. They met together to go to console and comfort him." Moreover, they had the initial good sense to sit "with him on the ground seven days and seven nights, and no one spoke a word to him, for they saw that his suffering was very great" (2:11–13).

The prologue has completed its task once Job's palpable affliction has brought this archetypal figure down to earth. For the earth he inhabits with us is the Lord's, as the setting of the story suggests in fairytale fashion; yet Job's response to his affliction will proceed to teach us how the Creator is present in ways that outstrip both intentional fairytale and purported theology. Indeed, this story of a Gentile living far outside the land of Israel will nonetheless conform to that pattern of the Hebrew scriptures that literary folk insist on calling "naturalistic." That is, there is no palpable "divine intervention" in the ensuing drama until a voice is heard "from the whirlwind" at the very end, which will identify itself as divine yet for that very reason poses singular difficulties of interpretation. So we are left with a many-sided exchange among Job and his interlocutors: an exchange that includes God, but in a variegated way that allows each dialogue to contribute to the central deconstructive aim of the whole. Let us follow the sinuous paths of that interaction.

# 3

# Three Rounds
# of Multifaceted
# Dialogue

## 3.1. First Round

### *Eliphaz the Temanite—dogmatist*

Job initiates the conversation by "cursing the day of his birth" (3:1): "Let that night be barren; let no joyful cry be heard in it. . . . Let the stars of its dawn be dark; let it hope for light, but have none" (3:7, 9). "Why did I not die at birth, come forth from the womb and expire? . . . Why is light given to one who cannot see the way, whom God has fenced in? . . . What I dread befalls me, I am not at ease nor am I quiet" (3:11, 23, 25–26). Eliphaz, the dogmatist, will not tolerate such incoherent self-pity—were I not here, there would be nothing to protest!—so demands rhetorically: "Think now, who that was innocent ever perished?

Or where were the upright cut off?" (4:7). More than a few instances come readily to mind, of course, but Eliphaz proffers recurring axioms in the form of questions, for serious queries would contravene the sheer holiness of God: "Can a mortal be more right than God, a human being more pure than one's Maker?" (4:17). He does not hesitate to put himself forward as a counterpoint to Job's desolation: "As for me, I would seek God, and to God I would commit my cause" (5:8), though at this point he is content to regale them with the magnanimous deeds of God that the psalmist recounts and that resonate with biblical wisdom literature. Whether it be the marvels of nature or the reversals of human affairs—"he frustrates the devices of the crafty so that their hands achieve no success, . . . but he saves the needy from the sword of their mouth, from the hand of the mighty" (5:13, 15). These features of God's action embolden him to make more direct reference to Job: "How happy is the one whom God reproves; therefore do not despise the discipline of the Almighty. For he wounds, but he binds up; he strikes, but his hands heal. He will deliver you from six troubles; in seven no harm shall touch you" (5:17–19). Eliphaz purports to know all about the ways of the Lord, yet axioms distilled from traditional narratives carefully avoid addressing Job's plight. He addresses Job himself only obliquely, never addressing, but only talking about, God. Job does not fail to note that it is God who has fenced him in; for Eliphaz, he rather needs to be reminded that God's ways are always just, despite appearances to the contrary. A familiar ploy of theodicy!

In what could be regarded as a poetic masterstroke, Job continues to ventilate as though Eliphaz had not even spoken, for how else can one hope to meet such insensitive ploys? Yet while he may be able to dismiss Eliphaz's rhetoric, he frankly despairs of meeting the challenge of affliction at God's hands: "Let God decide and crush me, let him loose his hand and cut me off! . . . In truth I have no help in me, and any resource is driven from me" (6:9, 13). Wearied by Eliphaz's insouciance regarding his obvious plight, he challenges all three of them in words guaranteed to elicit their ire: "one supplicates his friend for a favor, but he leaves him the fear of the Almighty" (6:14). Not only are their words empty; they have shown themselves to be so: "My companions are treacherous like the torrents, like ravines of torrents that pass away, . . . when it is hot, they vanish from their place. . . . For now, you have gone into nothing, you see my calamity, and are afraid" (6:15, 17, 21). Nor had he sought any help from them: "Have I said, 'Make me a gift'? Or, 'From your wealth offer a bribe for me'? Or, 'Save me from my opponent's hand'? Or 'Ransom me from the hand of oppressors'?" (6:22–23).

Then he abruptly turns his back on them to address the Lord in a completely different tone: "Teach me, and I will be silent; make me understand how I have gone wrong. . . . Will you consider words a proof and the speeches of a sufferer wind?" (6:24, 26). For that is how he feels with his friends arraying themselves against him. Yet turning to direct address emboldens him to speak more directly to God: "But now, be pleased to look at me; for I will not lie to your face. Turn, I pray, let no wrong be done. Turn now, my right is at stake. Is there any wrong on my tongue? Cannot my taste discern perversion?" (6:28–30). Inwardly freed from debating with his peers, he sets the tone for the rest of the book: "Therefore I will not restrain my mouth; I will speak in the anguish of my spirit; I will complain in the bitterness of my soul" (7:11). But the complaints no longer serve to punctuate self-pity; they are now directed to the very One whom he identifies as his persecutor: "Will you look away from me for a while, let me alone until I swallow my spittle? . . . Why have you made me your target? Why have I become a burden to you?" (7:19–20).

### Bildad the Shuhite—jurist

Bildad the jurist needs to defend the justice of God: "How long will you say these things, and the words of your mouth be a great wind? Does God pervert justice? Or does the Almighty pervert the right? . . . If you will seek God and make supplication to the Almighty, if you are pure and upright, surely then he will rouse himself for you and restore you to your rightful place. . . . God will not reject a blameless person, nor take the hand of evildoers" (8:2–3, 5–6, 20). Job's riposte acknowledges all this, and more, by altering the key: "Indeed I know that this is so; how can a mortal be right with God? If one wished to contend with him, one could not answer him once in a thousand. He is wise in heart and mighty in strength . . . who does great things beyond understanding, and marvelous things without number" (9:2–4, 10). Yet it is not justice that is primarily at issue, but the inequity in their relationship: "Look, he passes by me, and I do not see him; he moves on, but I do not perceive him. He snatches away; who can stop him? Who will say to him: 'What are you doing?' . . . How then can I answer him, choosing my words with his? Though I am right, I cannot answer him, I must supplicate for my right. If I summoned him that he would answer me, I do not believe he would listen to my voice. . . . If it is a contest of strength, he is the strong one!

If it is a matter of justice, who will plead for me?" (9:11–12, 14–16, 19).

Then in a shift of direction, Job seems rather to be addressing God more directly, through ending with a third-person plea: "If he would take his rod away from me, and not let dread of him terrify me, then I would speak without fear of him; as it is not so, I am left to myself" (9:34–35). Yet that fact does not deter him: "I will give free utterance to my complaint; I will speak in the bitterness of my soul" (10:1). Indeed, precisely because he sees himself standing in a relationship, however unequal, he does not hesitate to address God directly: "Do not condemn me; let me know why you contend against me. . . . Your hands fashioned and made me; and now you turn and destroy me" (10:2, 8). So he does not feel himself to be contending with sheer power: "You have granted me life and steadfast love, and your care has preserved my spirit" (10:12). The intimation here, though cast in terms of power, attends any attempt to remind us of God's justice: it will be quite beside the point, since divine justice cannot be expected to conform to our norms. "If I am wrong, woe is me! Even if I am right, I cannot lift up my head, for I am filled with disgrace and look upon my affliction" (10:15). Yet withal, Job's daring to address directly the source of his affliction and of the universe suggests another path than that of justice, which taken in itself is bound to fail, given the relation of creatures to their creator.

### Zophar the Naamathite—philosopher

Zophar, the philosopher, now enters the fray, convinced he can cinch the "first round": "Can you find out the deep things of God? Can you find out the limit of the Almighty? It is higher than heaven—what can you do? Deeper than Sheol—what can you know?" (11:7). Yet he cannot forbear enunciating a few axioms as well, presuming (as he must) that they pertain to "the deep things of God": "If you direct your heart rightly, surely then you will lift up your face without blemish, and you will be secure, and will not fear. . . . But the eyes of the unjust ones will fail; all way of escape will be lost to them, and their hope is to breathe their last" (11:13, 15, 20). Zophar is simply reminding Job that his fate lies in his hands: he alone can determine whether he is just or unjust. Job's explosion at such idle reminders prepares a transition to the "second round": "No doubt you are the people, and wisdom will die with you. But I have understanding as well as you; I am not inferior to you. Who does not know such things as these? I have become the one who is a laughingstock to his friend, who calls God that he may answer him, a laughingstock being right and blameless. . . . [indeed] the tents of robbers are at peace, and those who provoke God are secure, those whom God provided by his hand" (12:2–4, 6).

Of course God's wisdom surpasses anything we take to be wisdom: "Ask animals, and they will teach you; the birds of the air, and they will tell you. . . . Who among all these does not know that the hand of the Lord has done this?" (12:7, 9). For "with Him are wisdom and strength; he has counsel and understanding. . . . He uncovers the deeps out of darkness, and brings deep darkness to light. He makes nations great, then destroys them; he enlarges nations, then leads them away. He strips understanding from the leaders of the earth, and makes them wander in a trackless waste" (12:13, 22–24). Yet in the face of such overpowering wisdom, Job is the one "who calls

God that he may answer him" (12:4), and in that respect cannot but surpass his friends in wisdom: "I would speak to the Almighty, and I desire to argue my case with God. As for you, you apply false poultices, all of you are worthless physicians. If only you would keep silent, that would be your wisdom!" (13:3–5). (An allusion, *avant la lettre*, to Wittgenstein!) More provocatively, "Let him slay me, I do not hesitate, I will defend my ways to his face. . . . I have indeed prepared my case; I know that I shall be right" (13:15, 18). Now he can come to the point, directing his central request to God: "Only grant two things to me, then I will not hide myself from your face: withdraw your hand far from me, and do not let dread of you terrify me. Then call, and I will answer; or let me speak, and you reply to me" (13:20–22).

Noting how this request punctuates the surrounding rhetorical context in its directness and its simplicity, I take it to be the heart of the drama, addressed as it is directly to God. It is followed by a set of healthy reminders of the mortality Job shares with us all, culminating in the query: "If a mortal dies, will he live again?" (14:14), yet sustained by his insistence: "All the days of my service will wait until my release comes. You will call, and I will answer you; you will provide for the work of your hands" (14:14–15). It would be folly to try to predict when this will happen: "For now you number only my steps, . . . but the mountain falls and crumbles away, and the rock is removed from its place; the waters grind the stones; the torrents wash away the soil of the earth; so you destroy the hope of mortals. You prevail forever against him, and he passes away" (14:16, 18–20). So ends the first round. Everyone and everything is leveled by their relation to the Almighty, yet Job alone dares to address him.

## 3.2. Second Round

### Eliphaz the Temanite

Chastened to a sharper focus, Eliphaz no longer contents himself with repeating dogmatic assertions but attacks Job directly after an initial touch of self-irony: "Should the wise answer with windy knowledge, and fill himself with the east wind? Should he argue in unprofitable talk, or in words with which he can do no good?" (15:2–3). His retort pointedly turns Job's strident challenges to God into accusations impugning the Lord's wisdom and sovereignty: "Why does your heart carry you away, and why do your eyes flash, so that you turn your spirit against God, and let such words go out of your mouth?" (15:12–13). By turning Job's very affliction into an accusation, he aligns himself with "what sages tell, and have not hidden from the time of their ancestors" (15:18), coolly observing that "the unjust writhes in pain all his days" (15:20), with the explanation, "Because he has stretched forth his hand against God, and bids defiance to the Almighty" (15:25). Dogmatically inclined as he is, Eliphaz cannot discern a cry of pure anguish, so must translate Job's fulminations *to* God as claims *against* Him that pretend a justice superior to that of the Creator; so he proceeds to excoriate Job personally: "Let him not trust in emptiness, deceiving himself; for emptiness will be his recompense" (15:31). Job reacts by lashing out at all of them: "I have heard many such things; miserable comforters are you all. Have windy words no limit? Or, what troubles you that you keep on talking?" (16:2–3). But he concedes: "I would also talk as you do, if you were in my place; I would conjure against you by words, and shake my head at you" (16:4). So they are not the ones with whom he must take issue: "God gives me up to the knave, and casts me into the hands of unjust men. . . . It is his archers who surround me" (16:11, 13). Yet for all that, "even now, in fact, my witness is in heaven, and he that vouches for me is on high. My messengers are my cries, my eye pours out tears to God" (16:19–20). Yet just because his affliction is indescribable—"my spirit is broken, my days are extinct, the grave is ready for me. Surely there are mockers around me, and my eye dwells on their provocation" (17:1–2)—he cannot forswear his friends: "But you, come back now, all of you, though I cannot find a sensible person among you" (17:10). Their presence, at least, might alleviate his stark prospect: "Where then is my hope? Who will see my hope? Will it go down to the bars of Sheol? Shall we descend together into dust?" (17:15–16). In the end, the plight of his friends is no different from his own; another reason for needing their presence to mark a shared sense of inevitable oblivion.

### Bildad the Shuhite

Resuming the conversation on a resentful note—"Why are we counted as cattle? Why are we stupid in your sight?" (18:3)—Bildad, the jurist, finds that Job's complaints militate against the very order of things. "You who tear yourself in your anger—shall the earth be forsaken because of you, or the rock removed out of its place?" (18:4). Yet since that order so obviously obtains, we can only infer that "the light of the unjust one is put out, and the flame of his fire does not shine" (18:5). Graphically describing how the order of the universe becomes subverted for the unjust, with lightly veiled reference to Job's affliction—"by disease his skin is consumed" (18:13)—he concludes: "Surely such are the dwellings of the unjust man, such is the place of him who does not know God" (18:21). However tried-and-true Bildad's perspective may be, it misses its mark in Job, whose direct complaint to his companions underscores his own pain and their irrelevance: "How long will you torment me, and break me in pieces with words? . . . Know that God has bent me, and closed his net around me" (19:2, 6). So he saves his riposte for his primary tormentor, belying Bildad's parting inference that Job himself "does not know God," with a scathing complaint envisaging the divine tormentor himself: "He breaks me down on every side, I perish, he has uprooted my hope like a tree. . . . All my intimate friends abhor me, and those whom I loved have turned against me" (19:10, 19). With a plaintive plea to them, he manages: "Have pity on me, have pity on me, O you my friends, for the hand of God has touched me! Why do you, like God, pursue me?" (19:21–22). But apparently they can think of nothing else to do, so he turns from them to address the One whom he knows to be his primary tormentor, in a memorable confession that leaves complaint far behind: "I know that my redeemer is living, and rising the last on the earth! And then my skin will shake off this scab, and from my flesh I shall see God. That is what I see myself, my eyes have perceived and no other, my heart has concluded in my breast" (19:25–27). A broken bodily heart yields untoward wisdom, endowing him with the courage to warn his friends presciently: "Fear the sword for yourselves, for offence is a guilt deserving the sword, that you may know that there is a judgment" (19:29).

### Zophar the Naamathite

The best that Zophar can manage is a slim "theological reflection" reminding us "that the exulting of the unjust ones is short, and the joy of the infractor but for a moment" (20:5), as all leads to the judgment: "This is the unjust man's portion from God, the heritage decreed for him by God" (20:29). This exercise in analytic redundancy inspires Job to begin the third round with verve and confidence.

Daring to suggest that the very One whom he has been intent to confront is in fact the source of that daring—"Is it I who urges my reflection upon a man, or why have I not become weary?" (21:4)—Job admonishes his friends, "Listen carefully to my words, and let this be your consolation. Bear with me, and I will speak; then after I have spoken, mock on" (21:2–3). Since he no longer needs their "consolation," which has degenerated into a mockery, perhaps he can console them even while "shuddering seizes [his] flesh" (21:6). He devotes himself to offering an empirical challenge to Zophar's axiomatic insistence, which presumes to mirror the designs of the Creator, that the just will be rewarded and the unjust punished. For in fact, however considerably destinies may differ, the difference turns not at all on whether the principals have been just or unjust. Indeed, after a fulsome description of the way "the unjust live on, reach old age, and grow mighty in power" (21:7), Job can only conclude: "One dies in full prosperity, being wholly at ease and secure, his loins full of milk and the marrow of his bones moist. Another dies in bitterness of soul, never having tasted of good. They lie down alike in the dust, and the worms cover them" (21:23–26). The insistence of those intent

on preserving God's justice in axiomatic terms shipwrecks on
the facts of human history.

## 3.3. Third Round

### Eliphaz the Temanite

Such a stark denial of that retribution scheme that each
of his companions presents as the distillation of traditional
wisdom cannot but elicit a sharp rebuttal from the dogmatist,
Eliphaz. Prefacing with, "Is not your wickedness great? There
is no end to your guilt" (22:5), he goes on to rewrite the life
story that God had recounted to Satan to laud Job—"There is
no one like him on earth, a blameless and upright man who
fears God and turns away from evil" (2:3), insisting rather that
"you have sent widows away empty, and heavy hands crushed
the orphans" (22:9). Emboldened by this revised history, he
turns to address Job directly: "Will you keep to the old way
that the wicked have trod?" (22:15). Once having defended the
ironclad principles of the retribution scheme by falsifying Job's
life story, Eliphaz has only to admonish him: "Agree with God,
and be at peace, in this way good will come to you" (22:21).
But of course, to "agree with God" Job must agree with the
past that Eliphaz has invented, which would involve consent-
ing to a lie to save these time-honored principles. But in that
eventuality, the reward for such a "return to the Almighty" by
which Job "will be restored" (21:23) would have to be a justified condemnation. The framing legal irony of the book escapes
the dogmatist, whose deliberate recasting of Job's own story
mimics those self-justifying strategies endemic to ideologues
in every time and place.

In the face of such a maneuver Job cannot but return to himself: "Today also my complaint is bitter, and my hand checks my groaning" (23:2). But far from being self-enclosed, Job's complaint includes his primary interlocutor: "Oh, that I knew where I might find him, that I might come even to his seat! I would lay my case before him, and fill my mouth with arguments. I would know the words he would answer me, and understand what he would say. Would he contend with me in the greatness of his power? No, but he would give heed to me. There an upright person can reason with him, and I should carry forever my right" (23:3–7). Job has not utterly rejected his interlocutors' principles; his "uprightness" will stand him in good stead with God, but he moves leagues ahead of them precisely by seeking a personal audience. Yet for that to happen, the Creator must reveal himself to Job: yet, he says, "if I go forward, he is not there; or backward, I cannot perceive him" (23:8). However: "Since he knows the way to me, let him test me, I shall come out like gold" (23:10). Nevertheless, says Job, "I am terrified at his presence; when I consider, I am in dread of him. God has made my heart faint; the Almighty has terrified me" (23:15–16). Consumed by the dire need to present his case, yet also terrified at the prospect, Job can only await a response to his crucial plea: "Only grant two things to me, then I will not hide myself from your face: withdraw your hand far from me, and do not let dread of you terrify me. Then call, and I will answer; or let me speak, and you reply to me" (13:20–22). For the present he can go no further; yet should that plea be answered, he will also discover how wrong is his key presumption here: "I would know the words he would answer me, and understand what he would say" (23:5). His confidence will need to be further tempered if he is to find wisdom. Nor can he resist, at this point, turning his friends' accusations onto them to predict their demise, once more acceding to their general principles that injustice will be punished. Yet one suspects that his confidence is gleaned not from these principles themselves but from what he has come to know, through affliction, of their personal source.

### Bildad the Shuhite

Bildad briefly reiterates the principle that all jurists would have to acknowledge in the face of the Creator of heaven and earth: "How then can a mortal be right with God?" (25:4), so effectively undermines Job's aspiration to confront his creator and persecutor. Yet Job can hardly accept such a stark challenge to his program, so the "dialogue" (such as it has been) breaks down, leaving no further room for a theological rebuttal from Zophar. Indeed, the impasse reveals the fruitlessness of their exchange, as Job's interlocutors continue to adhere to a scheme of automatic retribution in the face of Job's confession of innocence, advancing an impersonal scheme against Job's forthright complaint. So the breakdown dramatizes the point of the book: an intertextual critique of an impersonal appropriation of the covenant scheme taken from Deuteronomy, whose original personal context has been intensified by Job's direct appeal to the author of the covenant. The chapters immediately following will bolster the grounds for that direct appeal.

### Job's final speech (with ode to Wisdom)

Job begins his parting words, extending over the next six chapters (26–31), with a stinging rebuke to his companions:

"How you have helped one who has no power! . . . How you have counseled one who has no wisdom, and given much good advice!" (26:2–3). Then he turns abruptly to avow the utter sovereignty of God : "Sheol is naked before God, . . . he stretches out Zaphon over the void, and hangs the earth upon nothing. . . . By his spirit the heavens were made pleasing . . . [and] these are indeed but the outskirts of his ways; and how small a whisper do we hear of him! But the thunder of his power who can understand?" (26:6–7, 13–14). Only then does he reiterate his intentions in the face of his friends' contentions, by a series of challenges in the form of oaths, beginning with "as long as my breath is in me and the spirit of God is in my nostrils, my lips will not speak falsehood. . . . Far be it from me to say that you are right; until I die I will not put away my integrity from me" (27:3–5). Moreover, this avowal emboldens him to turn the tables on them: "I will teach you concerning the hand of God; what is with the Almighty I will not conceal. Behold, all of you have seen it yourselves; why then do you annihilate it?" (27:11–12). If they are so knowledgeable regarding divine things, they cannot be ignorant of the way God will treat those who speak wrongfully of him as they have, indeed, "the heritage which oppressors receive from the Almighty" (27:13). After divine retribution described in vivid detail—"terrors overtake him like a flood; in the night the whirlwind carries him off" (27:20), we are treated to an ode to wisdom.

Couched in a geological idiom, the search for wisdom is likened to a mining excavation into the heart of the earth: "For there is a mine for silver, and a place for gold which they refine" (28:1). Yet daunting as it is to penetrate the bowels of the earth, Job reminds them that the wisdom we all seek is unattainable: "but where shall wisdom be found? And where is the place of understanding? Man does not know its space, and it is not found in the land of the living. . . . Whence then comes wisdom: and where is the place of understanding?" when none but the Creator "understands the way to it, and [only] he knows its place (28:12, 23). This One who orders all that is "saw it and declared it; he established it, and searched it out. And said to man, 'Behold, the fear of the Lord, that is wisdom; and to depart from evil is understanding'" (28:27–28). So a wisdom that is quite unattainable, in the sense that those who try to enunciate it only show themselves to be foolish, may nonetheless be bestowed upon those who act properly. Far from that which his friends claim to possess, it is this wisdom that Job seeks to gain from its very source by demanding an audience. Yet by identifying that demand with "fear of the Lord," Job will require his friends to transform their categories once again. Yet not even Job's rhetorical power can hope to effect such a conversion, so the performative logic that his comportment has introduced will demand nothing short of a response from the Lord himself. If Job's friends know not how to care for him, he can nonetheless hope that the Creator's resolution of his dilemma will serve also to bring them to a wisdom beyond the ersatz variety that has blocked their way to the genuine article.

Here Job cannot refrain from indulging in a self-pitying retrospective: "Oh, that I were as in the months of old, as in the days when God watched over me. . . . I put on righteousness, and it clothed me; my justice was like a robe and a turban. . . . Men listened to me, and waited, and kept silence for my counsel" (29:2, 14, 21). "But now they make sport of me, men who are younger than I, whose fathers I would have disdained to set with the dogs of my flock. . . . A senseless and disreputable brood, they have been whipped out of the land. . . . They abhor me, they keep aloof from me; they do not hesitate to spit at the sight of me" (30:1, 8, 10). And as if *lèse-majesté* were not bad enough, his demands are being spurned by God as well: "I cry to you and you do not answer me; I stand and you merely look at me. You have turned cruel to me; with the might of your hand you persecute me" to the point where "my skin turns black and falls from me, and my bones burn with heat" (30:20–21, 30). Yet in his affliction Job continues to avow the principles of his friends while resisting their applicability to his own case, noting that all this is taking place though he has acted consistently from "fear of the Lord." Recounting his exemplary conduct in the face of Eliphaz's deceitful revision of his life story, he presents case after case as a challenge to the Creator's own conduct toward him: "If I have walked with falsehood, . . . let me be weighed in a just balance, and let God know my integrity" (31:5–6). But these multiple self-justifications culminate in a heartfelt plea: "Oh, that I had one to hear me! Here is my signature! Let the Almighty answer me; and write a document, my adversary!" (31:35). With a solemn avowal that he is ready to undergo the punishment fitting anyone falsely presuming on the Creator's benevolence: "if I do not carry it [Job's signature, the judge's document] on my shoulder," Job reiterates that he will nonetheless "proclaim it in my every step" (31:36, 37) and then ceases to speak. At this dramatic impasse, Elihu steps forward to make up for the lack of wisdom of his elders.

Though some interpreters of the book of Job find that his reflections significantly alter the dramatic tension of the impasse between Job and his interlocutors, we shall rather find Elihu's discourse serving to heighten that impasse, precisely by presuming he can find a way through it. Readers of Job over the centuries have found Elihu's intervention baffling in different ways, leading some modern interpreters to suspect a later interpolation. As a way of suggesting the role Elihu plays in the poem, Jurij Bizjak poses this question: "Are the human intellect and experience able to add something more before the appearing of God?" (Bizjak 1991, 89). That suggestion makes ironic narrative sense, as we shall see, whatever one may think of the success of this final venture. Furthermore, by insisting on Elihu's youth, the author might wish to heighten a critique of that wisdom conventionally attributed to elders. In this way we shall find his extended discourse intensifying the impasse, as well as initiating the denouement, to bring us to the transcendent closure of the drama: the voice from the whirlwind.

# 4

# DENOUEMENT
# AND EPILOGUE

## Elihu's extended intervention

Elihu is indeed young, as he himself avers in a lengthy self-introduction, explaining how he has waited until his elders spoke before even daring to open his mouth. But now he must: "My heart is indeed like wine that has no vent; like new wine-skins, it is ready to burst. I must speak, so that I may find relief; I must open my lips and answer" (32:19–20). Yet once on stage, he is hardly at a loss for words: he first addresses Job (33), then his friends (34), then both together (35), and finally Job for a second and last time (36–37). Yet given that Job and his friends are at an impasse—Job's demand to confront God is as yet unconsummated, while his friends' theories have been rendered nugatory—Elihu opens by revealing his lack of wisdom as he fails to grasp the point of that impasse: the "fear of the Lord" that prevents anyone from claiming to be wise, yet enjoins upon each human being to seek it. "But now, hear my speech, O Job, and listen to all my words. . . . I will answer you; God is greater than any mortal. Why do you contend against him that he does not answer to any of the words applied to him?" (33:1, 12–13). Indeed, we seek in vain for any incisive pronouncements, and he even presumes to close his initial homily to Job by insisting: "if you have anything to say, answer me; speak for I desire to give you right. If not, listen to me; be silent, and I will teach you wisdom" (33:32–33). Wisdom, we want to aver (with Socrates), can hardly be taught!

Elihu does better when he takes on Job's friends for insisting that he must have done something wrong, reminding them how Job himself "has said, I am right, and God has taken away my justice" (34:5). Yet he can find little original to add to their theories: "For according to the work of a man [God] requites him, and according to his ways he makes it befall him. In truth, God does not do wrong, and the Almighty does not pervert justice" (34:11–12). He even closes by catering to them: "Men of understanding will say to me, and the wise man who hears me: 'Job speaks without knowledge, his words are without insight'" (34:34–35); and he explicitly associates himself with the friends whom he is addressing: "We pray, let Job test himself to the end for answering like evildoers. For he adds to his error, he excites the transgression among us, and multiplies his words against God" (34:36–37). Addressing them all in what follows, he forcibly recalls God's transcendence: "Look at the heavens and see; observe the clouds high above you. If you err, what do you accomplish against him? And if your transgressions are many, what do you do to him?" (35:5–6). He then unconsciously indicts himself by clearly missing the self-reference in his jibe at Job: "Job opens his mouth in empty talk, he multiplies words without knowledge" (35:16). To this point, one cannot but feel the author of Job responding to Jurij Bizjak's suggested query—whether the human intellect and experience are able to add something more before the appearing of God—with a canny negative: let a youth speak, and we will see that there is little wisdom worth reckoning there either.

As if to confirm that assessment of his intervention, Elihu addresses Job with a final rush of words, not hesitating to assume God's place: "Bear with me a little and I will show you, for I have something to say on God's behalf" (36:2). "God thunders wondrously with his voice; he does great things that we cannot comprehend" (37:5). "Hear this, O Job, stop and consider the wondrous works of God" (37:14). But Job (with his friends) has never ceased to do that; what he longs for is to hear that voice respond to his. Yet this may well mark the role Elihu's jejune preachments play in the drama: to prepare us to recognize that voice in the dramatic closure of this inner journey: "Listen to the message in the thunder of his voice and the rumbling that comes from his mouth" (37:2), for this is the One whose commands order and conserve all that he creates, as Elihu's closing words forcibly remind us.

## The "voice from the whirlwind"

The "voice from the whirlwind" takes the form of a two-part response by the Lord to Job's demands, punctuated with two brief ripostes from Job to maintain the semblance of a conversation. Before endeavoring to interpret the divine message, we should have been alerted to the overwhelming fact that "the Lord answered Job out of the whirlwind" (38:1). And though we are not told so, we may presume that God lifted his afflicting hand at the same time, thereby answering both Job's pleas: "Withdraw your hand far from me, and do not let dread of you terrify me. Then call, and I will answer; or let me speak, and you reply to me" (13:20–22). Indeed, it could even be that the overwhelming fact of God's response effectively eclipsed his affliction, much as alert readers of the Gospel of John will note how Jesus's very appearance to "doubting Thomas" rendered nugatory Thomas's carefully crafted criteria of verification, as John rejects Jesus's invitation to execute the criteria with a spontaneous confession of faith: "My Lord and my God!" (John 20:28). The response Job has sought from the outset consummates the drama, though again the terms of the Creator's *call* will elicit an *answer* from Job of a sort that he could never have anticipated.

We are all familiar with the tenor of the Creator's response, but focusing on what is purportedly said could easily distract us from the crucial fact that God indeed accepts Job's challenge to the Lord to address him directly, responding insistently: "Gird up your loins like a man, I will question you, and you shall declare to me" (38:3). Only then comes the cosmic putdown: "Where were you when I laid the foundations of the earth?" (38:4), which continues unrelentingly: "Have you comprehended the expanse of the earth? Declare, if you know all this" (38:18). The splendid proliferation of living things bears unceasing witness to the wisdom of the Creator, in the face of which Job only dares stammer: "See, I am too small; what shall I answer you? I lay my hand on my mouth, I cannot answer; therefore I will not speak twice" (40:4–5). Nevertheless, the Creator begins addressing him again, only to repeat the challenge: "Gird up your loins like a man . . ." (40:7), introducing Behemoth and Leviathan, as if to rub in the massive disproportion of scale between Job and his creator. Hardly lost on Job, he can but reply: "I know that you can do all things, and that no purpose of yours can be thwarted. . . . Therefore I declare that I do not understand things too wonderful for me, which I do not know" (42:2, 3). Yet he then insists, in a direct address somewhat reflective of the Lord's opening gambit ("Hear, and I will speak; I will question you, and you declare to me"), suggesting that the fact of being addressed directly by the Creator has more emboldened than belittled him: "I had heard of you by the hearing of the ear, but now my eye has seen you" (42:4–5). Now readers associated with the covenant of Moses know that no one can see the Lord and live; moreover, Job has heard, not seen. Yet his hearing is not like that of his friends; that is, he is not repeating what he has heard from others, for he has heard the Lord address him personally, which is much more like seeing! (At the end of a set of cryptic remarks, published as *Zettel*, the philosopher Ludwig Wittgenstein asserts: " 'You can't hear God speak to someone else, you can hear him only if you are being addressed'—that is a grammatical remark!" [1967, #717]) So like Abraham, who unmistakably recognized the One personally addressing him to be God, Job can retire from the fray humbly and with dignity: "Therefore I retreat and I repent in dust and ashes" (42:6).

## Epilogue

Job's fans will rejoice that God stoops to address his erstwhile friends as well, specifically Eliphaz, only to enjoin them to "offer up for yourselves a burnt offering; and my servant Job shall pray for you, for I will accept his prayer not to deal with you according to your folly; for you have not spoken of me what is right, as my servant Job has done" (42:8). This vindication of Job himself culminates the drama of Job and his friends in divine fashion, while the framing narrative closes as it began: "And the Lord restored the fortunes of Job when he had prayed for his friends; and the Lord gave Job twice as much as he had before" (42:10). Now for those of us who have followed the suspense of the drama, this serendipitous announcement can only be anticlimactic, for God had already answered Job, and done so directly. Yet the closing words, "and Job died, old and full of days" (42:17), return us to the promises of the Hebrew scriptures attending "the just," showing how this text that sets out to dismiss their misappropriations also vindicates their overall perspective. Which invites us to pursue the question, does Job offer a theodicy? If so, of what sort? If not, how can it lead us to some understanding of the ways of God toward us? And finally, can the understanding to which it intends to lead us be called a "theodicy," or must we find another term to present it? By following the contours of these questions, we may come to see these as far more than verbal issues, as we come to appreciate how the operative structure of the book of Job can lead us into yet more profound theological analysis, and so help us unravel conundra that can easily threaten religious convictions. Yet is that not what one ought rightly expect of a "theological reflection" on scripture: that it eschew a procrustean reduction of the issues to available categories, but rather attend to the ways revelation can expand and add nuance to the very strategies of theological reflection itself?

## 5

# A COMPARATIVE GLANCE AT AYYUB IN THE QUR'AN

## BY A. H. JOHNS

W E MENTIONED AT the outset of this reflection that there was no revelatory document in Islam comparable to the book of Job; that is, an extended narrative that presented a view of the Creator's interaction with creatures—in this case, a rational creature brought to dire extremity by the action, direct or indirect, of that very Creator. Furthermore, the interpersonal exchange within the drama is so pointed as to render nugatory, and even silly, standard justifications of the divinity's action constructed according to norms ostensibly articulated in other parts of the revelatory text itself. Indeed, this is what allows the book of Job

51

to subvert "clerical" interpretations of the Hebrew scriptures, whereby punishment so inevitably follows wrongdoing that any affliction can be read as a sign of divine punishment presupposing guilt on the part of the victim. The Qur'anic Job, however, cannot be encountered directly, as in the fulsome biblical narrative, but must rather be reconstituted from narrative snatches, as is often the case with the Qur'an. A faithful reconstruction demands consummate skills, not only cultural-linguistic, but literary as well. Anthony Johns has executed a series of such readings of figures known to Jews and Christians from the Bible who are also found in the Qur'an. By emending his study of Job for inclusion in this theological reflection on the Bible, readers can sample something of the relation of these two sources, each deemed revelatory by their respective communities, as well as come to appreciate the quality of sophistication demanded to read a Qur'anic text fruitfully. While the Qur'anic treatment lacks a sustained poetic complaint amply orchestrated by the dialectical harmonics of failed exchange with his interlocutors, Johns will show how this Job rather illustrates the recurring theme of the constancy of God's care for his creatures from the beginning of time by the sending of prophets. In presenting Job in the context of these divine interventions in human affairs, the Qur'an rather incorporates the figure of Job into the framework of a salvation history. Anthony Johns has a masterful way of showing us how effectively the Qur'an accomplishes its purpose with regard to the figure of Job, but this figure of Job is clearly subservient to that purpose.[1]

1. What follows abridges and adapts Johns's original essay "Narrative, Intertext and Allusion in the Qur'anic Presentation of Job," *Journal of Qur'anic Studies* 1 (1999): 1–25, by permission of the author.

The prophets in question are a specially chosen community, many of them known by name, others whose names were not divulged even to the Prophet Muhammad (4:162). A number of them, notably Abraham and Moses, have a commanding authority and self-evidently major role, others such as Joseph and Noah appear in fully fledged narratives, and yet others such as David and Solomon are presented in a number of vividly etched pericopes. Still others, however, are referred to comparatively briefly, their role and character defined and identified by a minimum of narrated information about them and words God addresses to them, or sets on their lips as direct speech. These "lesser" prophetic figures—lesser in relation to the space devoted to them, not to their importance—include Idris [Enoch] (19:56–57, 21:85), Dhu 'l-Kifl (21:85, 38:48), al-Yasa [Elisha] (6:86, 38:48), Ilyas [Elias] (6:85, 37:123–30, and possibly referred to in 18:65), Ayyub [Job] (4:163, 6:84, 21:83–84, 38:41–44), and Yunus [Jonah], also referred to as Dhu 'l-Nun and Sahib al-Hut (4:163, 6:86, 10:98, 21:87–88, 37:139–48, 37:139–48, 68:48–50).

They appear as vignettes, and have to the great figures of prophecy a role comparable to that of predella to major paintings in the visual arts. Assessed by the criteria of the number of episodes in which they play a role, frequency of mention, and the length and detail of the pericopes devoted to them, they are subsidiary to the great figures, yet while preaching the same message, present individual aspects of revealed truth and are integrated into the prophetic structure of the Qur'an by a variety of intermeshing literary conduits and devices. Frequency of mention and length of pericope, however, do not always coincide with the hierarchical order in which some traditions place them. When the Prophet was taken up to the seventh heaven on the night of the *miraj*, at each stage of his ascent he met one of his predecessors. At the fourth heaven he met Idris, who, with only two attestations, was ranked above Adam (at the first), Jesus and John (at the second), and Joseph (at the third), notwithstanding the multiple and extensive references to each of these and the entire chapter devoted to Joseph (Guillaume 1955, 185–86).

Although these six lesser prophets are well represented in *Qisas al-Anbiya* and are popular as personal names among male Muslims, they have attracted little interest outside the world of Islam. The pericopes in which they occur have not received much positive comment from Western scholars.[2] This essay is structured around Job [Ayyub] as one of these lesser prophets. Of the four pericopes in which he is mentioned, only two give narrative information about him, one in the space of four verses, and the other of two. The other two simply include his name among an assembly of prophets. Nevertheless, despite the brevity of these Qur'anic references, they have made a major contribution to the religious imagination and spirituality of the Muslim community documented in *tafsir*, in *Qisas al-Anbiya*, and in the mystical tradition (Ibn 'Arabi 1980, 212–17). They are discussed in order of revelation: 38:41–44 and 21:83–84 (which give narrative information), and 6:83–88

2. Lemmata dedicated to them in reference works, including the *Encyclopaedia of Islam* (both editions: EI1, EI2), are brief, and often more concerned with their identification in the Judaeo-Christian tradition than with their significance in the context of the Qur'an and the spiritual values they exemplify. By way of example, Arthur Jeffrey in his entry *Ayyoub* in EI2 regards the references to Job as "confused" and, by implication, of little interest: "Job is mentioned twice in the Kur'an in lists of those to whom Allah had given special guidance and inspiration (4:163/161, 6:84), and fragments of his story are given in 21:83–84; 38:41/40–44. . . . In the story of the miraculous spring by which he was healed, there seems to be a confusion with the Naaman story of II Kings V, and in the obscure verse about his taking a bundle in his hand and striking with it, there may be a similar confusion with the story in II Kings 12:14 ff" (EI 2: I. 795–796 *Ayyoub*).

and 4:163 (which present him only as a member of an assembly of prophets).

## I

A suggested rendering of the Sad (Sura 38) pericope is as follows:

> 41 And tell of Our servant Job,
> when he called his Lord,
> "Satan has indeed touched me with hardship and pain."
>
> 42 "Scuff [the earth] with your foot!
> "This is [a spring] a cool place to bathe,
> and [it is] drink."
> 43 We gave [back] to him his kinsfolk and the like of
>      them with them
> as a mercy from Us
> and as a lesson to those with understanding.
>
> 44 "Take in your hand a sprig [of leaves]
> and strike with it!
> Do not break an oath."
> Indeed We found him patient. How excellent a servant!
> He was turned constantly [to Us].

These verses may be regarded as a core statement of the prophetic experience of Job, which the other Qur'anic references to him complement or re-present. It is highly dramatic. God instructs Muhammad to tell of when Job called out in pain, presenting Job's words in direct speech. God's response to his call, in the form of a command, also in direct speech, follows immediately. Job's obedience to it is understood. God then, switching to narrative mode, tells a wider audience what he has done for Job and why. God then addresses Job with a second command. Again Job's obedience to it is understood. God, switching again to narrative mode, praises him, indicating the qualities by which he is distinguished.

Qur'anic language is condensed and allusive, and the extent and depth of meanings that the exegetical tradition discovers within it are not self-evident. The pericope is confronting and presents a challenge that could be perplexing, particularly since Job does not at first sight fit into the general prophetic mold. There is no account of his call, of divine words by which he is commissioned, the giving to him of a book, the people to whom he preached, their acceptance or rejection of him, or the punishment that would follow such a rejection. In fact, it is his example in bearing undeserved suffering that is his message. Despite, indeed because of, its brevity and allusiveness, there is a tautness and dramatic power in the language, deriving from the tension of undisclosed information. Who was Job? What led him to cry out in anguish? How did Satan bring hardship and pain upon him? Why was he told to scuff the ground? Why did he need the water? When and how was his family taken from him? Why was Job ordered to take a sprig of leaves to strike someone or something? What was the oath it is incumbent on him to keep? What is the connection between the two apparently unrelated parts of the pericope? And finally, why does God praise him so highly at the conclusion of the verse?

Questions like these invite us to ask how the first hearers of these verses understood them, profoundly conscious as they were that the words they were hearing were divine words. For the answer that they had for them, it is necessary to turn to the reports of the Companions and Followers as they have been passed on by the narratives relating words and actions of the Prophet (*hadiths*) and the *Qisas*. These are summarized in their fullest form by Tabari in his *Jami' al-Bayan* in three narrations—two deriving from Wahb bin Munabbih, one from al-Hasan al-Basri—that he includes in his exegesis. These allow him to expand the Qur'an's condensed presentation as follows. Satan, speaking to God, claims that Job, who is faithful to the Lord in prosperity, will not be faithful when he encounters adversity. God accordingly allows Satan to put Job to the test by destroying his property, by killing his livestock and members of his family, and then afflicting him with painful, repellent disease, so that all apart from his wife abandon him. Satan attempts to make Job waver in his faithfulness to God through his wife. Playing on her pity for him in his misery, Satan persuades her to urge him to sacrifice a kid to him. Job realizes that she has allowed herself to be taken in by Satan. He swears an oath to punish her with a hundred lashes if he recovers, and tells her to leave him. Totally alone after she has left, he cries to God in anguish, uttering the words: "Satan has indeed touched me with hardship and pain" (v. 41).

By putting together these reports, Tabari has established a context for the events mentioned or referred to in the verses, identified the dramatis personae, and clarified their spiritual and moral message. In the light of the background he provides, we can hear the compact language of the Qur'an presenting with deft strokes a vivid picture of the way Job, a prophet put to the test by the loss of his possessions, livestock, and family and by the physical suffering of disease, remained as faithful to God in hardship as he had been in prosperity without questioning God's wisdom. When he calls out in pain and loneliness after dismissing his wife, who has unwittingly been deceived by Satan, God answers him. He relieves his suffering with a spring of water to heal him and quench his thirst; out of his mercy he restores to him his family, and in addition the like of them with them. By his answer to Job's cry he makes of Job's patience and endurance a lesson "for those with understanding" (v. 43). He instructs him to take into his hand a sprig of a hundred leaves so that by one blow with it he would have struck his wife with the hundred lashes as he had sworn to do on his recovery, warning him not to break the oath he has made. He then praises Job

Given this background, the sense of the pericope is clear. Moreover, it is exquisitely structured. Not a word is wasted; even the interstices of silence between the utterances are fraught with meaning. Notwithstanding its brevity, the literary design is complex. It is in two parts: in one Job calls on his Lord for relief from the pain with which Satan has afflicted him, in the other God commands him to take a sprig of leaves and to strike a blow with it. Each includes a mix of narration and direct speech. In part one, Job cries aloud (direct speech); God responds giving an order (direct speech); God then speaks in narrative mode. In part two, God gives an order (direct speech), then speaks in narrative mode. A binary structure informs both parts. In part one, there are two components to God's response to Job, and each has likewise two parts. The spring is cleansing, it is also drink; Job's family is restored *and* the like of them with them; God's response is summated as a mercy *and* a lesson. But within these complementary binary structures, there are antitheses. Job suffers hardship and pain, the water brings cleansing and quenches thirst. Something harmful is removed, while something beneficent is put in its place. It is understood that Job's kin have been taken away; they are then brought back. There are parallels in the structure of part two. God's second command is likewise binary. Job is to do one thing (take a sprig and strike); he is to avoid doing another (break an oath).

The unity between the two parts is established in a number of other ways. In each there is a tension to be released: in part one the tension occasioned by Job's pain, in part two the possibility of the sin of a dishonored oath. Another is the chiasmus between the two commands: "Scuff with your *foot*" (v. 42) in part one, and "Take in your *hand*" (v. 44) in part two. Further, there is a symmetric distribution of double bipartite ellipses. In part one, Job's obedience to God's command to scuff the earth is understood, and likewise the healing that the water brings him. In the second, what is to be struck (his wife) and his obedience to the command are elided. The closing formula, "Indeed we found him patient. How excellent a servant! He was turned constantly [to Us]" (v. 44), is imbued with a verbal music that carries melodic tones of other formulae in praise of the prophets throughout the Qur'an. Finally, the appearance of the spring is especially significant. It carries echoes of other references in the Qur'an to the appearance of springs with life-giving water, and the death and disintegration that follows drought. God's order to Job to scuff the ground with his foot may be seen as a counterpart to his order to Moses: "Strike the rock with your staff" (7:160), to release the water that quenched the thirst of the Israelites. Indeed the appearance of the spring, with the image of a cleansing healing stream it evokes, dominates the scene. It is difficult not to see a reference to Job, with the healing spring that burst from the ground when he scuffed his foot at the divine command, in the ecstatic line of Rumi, "Whenever the lover touches the ground with his dancing feet, the water of life will spring out of the darkness" (quoted by Schimmel 1975, n. 183).

The immediate context of these verses referring to Job presents him as one of an assembly of prophets, thereby demonstrating that his prominence stems not from himself alone, but as part of a community of prophets, who at once share a common role and election, yet remain distinct from one another in their personalities and individual charisms. The variety of perspectives from which they are presented shows the richness of the prophetic vocation, which, with the distinctive emphasis of the divine message each one preaches, exemplifies and justifies Muhammad's own role and vocation. It will be worth attending to the details of this context, the better to delineate the specific role Job plays in it. The assembly of prophets with whom he is associated comprises Noah, Hud, Moses (v. 12), Salih, Lot, and Shu'ayb (v. 13), David (vv. 17–26), Solomon (vv. 30–40), Job himself (vv. 41–44), Abraham, Isaac, and Jacob (vv. 45–47), and Ishmael, Elisha, and Dhu 'l-Kifl (v. 48). This company is not given in a chronological order but ranges from the most frequently mentioned to the least, from Abraham and Moses to Elisha and Dhu 'l-Kifl.

This assembly is symmetrically structured into three groups: the first of six, (subdivided into two groups of three), the second of three, and the third of six (also subdivided into two groups

of three). Of the first group, no narrative information is given
other than that all the peoples to whom they were sent were
destroyed. Only two are mentioned by name, Noah and Lot.
The others are identified by the peoples to whom they were
sent: 'Ad, to whom Hud was sent; Thamud, to whom Salih
was sent; in the case of the Egyptians, by their leader Pharaoh,
to whom Moses was sent; and by residence, the people of the
thicket, that is, Midian, to whom Shu'ayb was sent. Emphasis
is here on the peoples destroyed for rejecting their prophets,
rather than on the prophets sent them. The second forms the
core group. It consists of David, Solomon, and Job. Narrative
information is given of each of them. Each has a different
charism. They differ from the first group in that none of them
is named as sent to a particular people with a specific message,
no one rejects them and is destroyed in punishment. They
likewise differ from each other.

David is presented as one "endued with strength, he was constantly turned [to Us]" (v. 17), as one with whom the hills and
birds were made to join in singing the praise of God (vv. 18–19).
His kingdom was made secure; he was given decisiveness in
speech. He is put to the test by two disputants who intrude
into his sanctuary (Johns 1989). For a fault revealed by, or
committed in the course of facing, that test, he repents/turns
again to God. He is given a reward: "Indeed he is close to Us,
and has a beautiful dwelling place" (v. 25). He is appointed
vicegerent and commanded to rule with justice. Solomon is
presented as David's son. He is described: "How excellent a
servant! He was constantly turned [to Us]" (v. 30). On one occasion when fine horses were paraded before him, he forgot the
performance of a prayer. As soon as he realized this fault, he had

them slaughtered so that never again would they distract him from his Lord. He was then put to the test by a figure placed on his throne.[3] For a fault that this test discloses, he repents, addressing God, "My Lord forgive me, and give me a kingdom such as none may have after me, you indeed are *the Bestower* (*al-Wahhab*)—a canonical "name of God" (Ghazali 1992). He is rewarded. The winds are made subject to him, and the demons put in servitude and made subject to him. This is God's gift. Of him too God says, "Indeed he is close to Us, and has a beautiful dwelling" (v. 40).

Job is presented without any introduction. Muhammad is told directly to transmit the words Job uttered when he called out in pain, what God said to him, and how he obeyed. God says of him, "Indeed We found him patient. How excellent a servant! He was constantly turned [to Us]" (v. 44). The pericope closes with a panorama of a further six prophets, like the first, divided into two groups of three: Abraham, Isaac, and Jacob, who are "possessed of strength and perception" (vv. 45–46), the chosen, the elect; and Ishmael, Elisha, and Dhu 'l-Kifl, also *of the elect*, thus bringing the pericope to an end with a resounding hymnodic close. Although grouped together, there are marked differences between these three prophets. David and Solomon are father and son, but have different charisms. Only David has mountains and hills sing in praise of God with him. Unlike Solomon, he does not address God directly with a request. He exchanges words only with the intruders who confront him. There is a difference in the tests to which Solomon and David

3. A common interpretation of this verse is that Solomon captured the daughter of the king of Sidon, and that since she grieved for her father so much, he had the demons at his service make an image of him to which she and her maid-servants paid homage, leading unwittingly to the tolerance of idolatry under his roof.

are put; likewise, there is a nuanced variation in the statement of their personal qualities: "David is endued with strength, he was constantly turned [to Us]," while of Solomon it is said: "How excellent a servant! He was constantly turned [to Us]" (v. 30). The contrast with Job could hardly be greater. There are no introductory phrases to identify him or to highlight his qualities. His words are a cry of pain. In contrast to Solomon, he makes no request; unlike David, he does not repent of any sin. God answers his cry with two commands, yet his obedience to both is omitted. The laudatory formulae bestowed on him follow rather than precede the account given of him.

Notwithstanding these differences, there are common elements in the vocabulary that define their qualities and their rewards that stress their community. While David is "endued with strength" and Solomon is "excellent [as] a servant," God says of both, "He was constantly turned [to Us]." They both receive the same reward, God saying of each of them: "Indeed he is close to Us, and has a beautiful dwelling" (vv. 25 and 40). By the same token, Abraham, Isaac, and Jacob echo David's quality of being "endued with strength [and] constantly turned [to Us]," while Job is honored by the same laudatory phrase as Solomon: "How excellent a servant! He was constantly turned [to Us]," the second half of which is also said of David. He is distinguished from the others in this pericope, because of him alone God says: "Indeed We found him patient" (v. 44). Further, the phrase "for those with understanding" (v. 43), describing those for whom God's design for him is a lesson, is perhaps a cue to the qualities exemplified by Abraham, Isaac, and Jacob, numbered among those "possessing strength and perception" (v. 45).

The pericope needs to be heard in the wider context of the
sura. The sura opens presenting a scene of the arrogance and
dissension of those to whom the prophet Muhammad is preaching, and the divine warning directed to them, "How many of
[former] ages have We destroyed before them! They cried out
[when destruction fell upon them] but then was no time for
deliverance" (v. 3). It presents some of the objections they make
to the vocation of Muhammad, answered by God's words of
scorn as he says to the prophet, ". . . do they have [charge of]
the treasure chests of the mercy of your Lord, *The Mighty (al-
'Aziz), the Bestower (al-Wahhab)*." This is followed by warnings
made from the examples of past peoples who had rejected the
prophets sent to them and been destroyed. In this early part of
the sura, there are two words that establish themes developed
later. The first is *nadaw* ("they cried out") in "They cried out
[when destruction fell upon them] but then was no time for
deliverance" (v. 3). This word does not occur again until Job's
call, presented with dramatic suddenness in the phrase "He cried
out to his Lord" (v. 41), presenting a message with stark clarity:
If the unbelievers cry out when punishment overwhelms them,
their cry is in vain. When a prophet (or a believer) enduring
suffering cries out, he is heard at once. Thus, when Job calls he is
given a healing spring, and what had been taken from him when
he was put to the test is restored. The second is the designation
of God as *al-Wahhab* (v. 9). The Meccans reject Muhammad
because they refuse to believe that a revelation be given to
one of themselves—they are astonished that a warner, one of
themselves, should come to them (v. 4). God proclaims that he
is *al-'Aziz*, the Mighty, *al-Wahhab*, the Bestower. In other words,
it is in his nature to give, and he can give the gift of prophecy to

whomever he wills. This quality of God as Bestower is reiterated through the sura. God *gave* David Solomon (v. 30). Solomon asks *to be given* a kingdom. When addressing God with a request, he appeals to him as *al-Wahhab* (v. 35). Power over the wind and the demons God says is "Our gift" to Solomon (v. 39). God *gave* back to Job what had been taken from him.

A feature of the structure of the sura is the alternation of passages referring to the Meccans, Muhammad's contemporaries, with passages relating to former prophets. Thus, after an account of the fate of past peoples who have been destroyed—the people of Noah, the tribe of 'Ad, and so on (vv. 12–13)—the Qur'an tells of the sneer of Muhammad's contemporaries when warned of the coming of a day of reckoning: "Lord of ours, give us our requittal now, before the day of reckoning" (v. 16), in face of which God commands the prophet, "Be patient in face of what they say" (v. 17), telling him to recall David, the first of the group of three prophets to which Job belongs. This word *isbir* is picked up in the words in praise of Job, "Indeed We found him patient (*sabiran*)" (v. 44), for patience/endurance is Job's special charism as a supreme model for Muhammad as he faces rejection by his people.

## II

The pericope from al-Anbiya' (21) may be rendered as follows:

> 83 And [tell too of] Job when he called his Lord
> "Hurt has indeed touched me
> though You are most merciful of the merciful."

> 84 We thereupon heard him, so removed what of hurt
> was upon him.
> We brought [back] to him his kinsfolk and the like of
> them with them
> as a mercy from Our presence
> and as a lesson to [Our] servants.

Like the previous pericope, it is introduced by the elliptical command to the prophet to recount Job's addressing his Lord. Job's words are given in direct speech. He calls, "Hurt (*durr*) has indeed touched me," and continues "though You are most merciful of the merciful." God then tells of his response to Job's cry, "We thereupon heard him, so removed what of hurt was upon him" (v. 84) and tells how he brought [back] to Job his kin and the like of them with them as a mercy and a lesson. It is briefer than the corresponding pericope in Sad. It echoes it, and the key words and phrases it repeats reinforce and enrich the hearers' memory of Job in the earlier (in order of revelation) pericope, and thereby heightens awareness of the presence of Job as a personality in the Qur'an. Heard together with the earlier pericope, it gives the episode a stereophonic and indeed stereoscopic dimension. Nevertheless, it has its own character established by variations that occur at the word and phrase level. They may be summarized as follows:

i "Hurt has indeed touched me," in place of "Satan has indeed touched me"

ii with "hurt" (*bi durrin*) in place of "with hardship and pain"

   iii  Additional phrase "Though You are most merciful of the merciful"

   iv  Omission of "Scuff with your foot"

    v  Additional phrase "We thereupon heard him, so removed what of hurt was upon him"

   vi  "We brought [back] to him" for "We gave him"

  vii  "from Our presence" for "from Us"

 viii  "to [Our] servants" for "to those with understanding"

   ix  Absence of second command

    x  Absence of laudatory formulae

So closely are the two presentations of the scene bonded, that variations at phrase level, the absences and additions, may be regarded as ellipses in the one and complements in the other. Thus, the juxtaposition of the additional phrase "though You are most merciful of the merciful," not occurring in Sad, is not inconsistent with the tone of the cry in Sad, and may well be considered as a complement, realizing an ellipsis. At the same time, its presence in al-Anbiya' suggests a different perspective to Job's cry, investing it with an element of reproach. For how or why should "the most merciful of the merciful" allow *hurt* to touch his servant?

Likewise, the divine command "Scuff with your foot" (38:42) may in al-Anbiya' be regarded as elliptical, whereas God's words, "We thereupon heard him, so lifted the hurt that was upon him," may be regarded as a complement, as he continues the narrative in al-Anbiya', supplying what is omitted in Sad. So just as the command "Scuff with your foot" is present in the minds of hearers of al-Anbiya' who know the Sad presentation, so "We thereupon heard him" is present in the minds of listeners to the Sad presentation of the scene. In others words, in Sad, the emphasis is on the means (the spring) by which God removed the *hardship* and *pain* that were upon Job, whereas in al-Anbiya' it is on God's removing the *hurt*. The word *hurt* (*durr*), together with *hardship* and *pain*, generalizes and internalizes the degree of Job's agony. In addition, it has a particular resonance in Qur'anic discourse, evoking an association with other verses that have to do with the power of God and the helplessness of idols, as in Abraham's riposte to his idolatrous compatriots: "Do you then worship in place of God what can neither help you nor hurt?" (21:66). Job's cry "Hurt has touched me" in place of "Satan has touched me . . ." shifts the agent of the act from Satan, yet short of accusing God of causing the pain, recognizes that only God can lift it. Thus, the way is opened for a different perspective on Job's suffering, and God's relationship to it.

Part two of the corresponding verses is not repeated, and the passage concludes with a nuanced reprise of the significance of the restoration of Job's kin, the lesson it teaches being "for [Our] servants," a variation leaving open the possibility for a different perspective and shift of emphasis. As in Sad, the immediate context of the Job verses is provided by an assembly of other prophets. They are Moses and Aaron (v. 48), Abraham (vv. 51–70), Lot (v. 71), Isaac and Jacob (vv. 72–73), Lot, again (vv. 74–75), Noah (vv. 76–77), David and Solomon (vv. 78–79), David (v. 80), Solomon (vv. 81–82), Job (vv. 83–84), Ishmael, Idris, and Dhu 'l-Kifl (vv. 85–86), Dhu 'l-Nun [Jonah] (vv. 87–88), Zechariah and John (vv. 89–90), Jesus son of Mary (v. 91). This assembly can be divided into two groups, those of whom God speaks directly, and those whom he commands

Muhammad to tell of. They may also be divided between those concerning whom narrative information, or at least an allusion to an event in their lives, is given, and those mentioned only by name but honored by laudatory formulae either as a preamble or a conclusion.

God himself speaking in narrative mode introduces the assembly of prophets. The pericope exhibits a variety of structural devices. One already mentioned distinguishes those prophets mentioned directly by God from those introduced by the words Muhammad is commanded to utter. Another discriminates those of whom we are given narrative information from those marked only by laudatory formulae. It is a device with considerable literary effect. Consider the narrative verses relating to Job: "He called to his Lord, 'Indeed hurt (*durr*) has touched me, though You are most merciful of the merciful'"(v. 83). God replies, "So We heard him and removed what was of hurt from him" (v. 84). Consider likewise those relating to Jonah: "He departs in fury, thinking We have no power over him. He called out in the darkness, "There is no God but You. Glory to You!" God answers, "So We heard him and saved him from oppression" (v. 87). And God adds, "In like manner so We save those who believe." These two vignettes are separated by the verse in praise of Ishmael, Idris, and Dhu 'l-Kifl (v. 85). Job and Jonah both cry out in anguish, and the verses devoted to each of them are of great emotional power. The intervening verse, one in praise of three other prophets, offers a brief relaxation of tension, and so doing adds to the impact of both. This verse, however, has an additional function. Ishmael, Idris, and Dhu 'l-Kifl are praised as being "all of the patient." In this sura, the Job verses make no mention of his patience, so evident in Sad

(38:44), "Indeed We found him patient." The phrase "all of the patient" occurring in the following verse serves as a cue to God's praise of Job's patience in Sad, and so by proxy associates it with him here too. This may be compared with the reference to the demons made subject to Solomon, and diving for him (v. 82). The name Satan [*shayatin*] may likewise be heard as a cue to the role of Satan in Job's cry in Sad, "Indeed Satan has touched me" (38:41), thereby drawing attention to the role of Satan in Job's suffering.

The prophets in this assembly differ from one another in personality as well as in their situations. Among them, Job, Jonah, and Zechariah form a typological group: they are not prophets who preach and are rejected yet then vindicated when punishment falls on those who rejected them, like Lot, Noah, and Moses. Neither are they prophet rulers like David and Solomon, nor do they play a role in a grand scheme of reconciliation and the righting of wrong, like Joseph. They are simply prophets who suffer. Yet they suffer in different ways and for different reasons. Even though each addresses God directly, each appeals to God in relation to his own needs. Job calls for relief from the hurt that has touched him—loss of property and family and suffering physical affliction; Jonah cries in darkness, frustrated that his people had rejected him; while Zechariah reveals his longing for an heir, for without a child of his own, his evil nephews would inherit from him and destroy his spiritual patrimony.

Despite their diversity, however, the prophets are marked as a community sharing formulae of praise distributed among them within the pericope, which also forms an organic part of the sura in which it is set, so the meaning of the pericope is enhanced and a further dimension disclosed when it is heard in this wider context. It opens with a warning of the coming of an eschatological moment (v. 1), and the disregard of humankind for such warnings (v. 2). It tells of the insults of those who reject the Prophet. "Is this other than a human being like yourselves" (v. 3), and ". . . he has made it up, he is a poet, so let him bring us a sign as did those who were formerly sent" (v. 5). It answers the objections made to Muhammad, telling of the destruction of previous peoples who had rejected the messengers sent to them, affirming that all these messengers too had been human, and as humans had needed food to live by, and that none of them were immortal (v. 8). From such points of departure, the sura articulates a number of general themes that are individualized in the prophets presented in the pericope. It proclaims that the message God has revealed to Muhammad and to every messenger before him is, "We have not sent any prophet before you without revealing to him that there is no God but I, so worship me" (v. 25), and the testimony to this is the cry of Jonah in the whale, "There is no god but You. Glory to You," by virtue of which God saves him from the darkness (v. 87). It proclaims God as the Merciful. The unbelievers are denounced because they claim the Merciful has taken a son (v. 26), and because they "disbelieve what is said of the Merciful" (v. 36). In rebuttal, Muhammad is commanded to warn them, "Who can guard you by day or night from the Merciful" (v. 42). And a proof of God's mercy is his answer to Job's call for relief from hurt (*durr*) as soon as he addresses God as "most merciful of the merciful." God's mercy is realized and proved by this response to Job, thereby highlighting the example of how one should appeal to him Job gives, and his consequent status among the prophets.

A further theme has humankind being put to the test. God addresses humankind, "We try you, putting you to the test, by evil and by good, and to Us you shall be returned" (v. 35). Job is the ultimate example of a prophet put to the test, and the Sad pericope tells how David and Solomon too were put to the test (38:24 and 34). Yet although God puts individuals to the test, he is a saving God. When his prophets are in difficulties or danger, he saves them. This is enunciated clearly, God proclaiming, "We were true to Our promise to them, so We saved them [from those who rejected them] together with whomever We willed [to save], and We destroyed the wicked" (v. 9). The verse makes the general statement that God is faithful to his promise [to his prophets]. In the pericope in which Job has his place are individual examples of God acting as faithful to his promise to save. He saves Abraham (v. 71), Lot (v. 74), Noah (v. 76), and Jonah (v. 88). He lifts the hurt from Job (v. 84), and he gives Zechariah a son (v. 90). There are numerous direct and indirect links between the earlier part of the sura and the prophetic pericope. Another example is to be seen in two verses telling how the evildoers react when they feel God's punishment, "Behold, they scuff the ground in flight from it" (v. 12), and God orders them with biting sarcasm: "Do not scuff the ground in flight . . ." (v. 13). The Job verses in this sura do not present the divine command to Job in Sad, "Scuff with your foot," which may be regarded as omitted in this more concentrated presentation of the scene, yet the negative command to the evildoers *Do not scuff* suggests the positive command to Job *Scuff with your foot*. This would allow hearers of the Qur'an to realize the ellipsis, so appreciate the different destiny of the good and the wicked by contrasting

those who scuff the ground in flight and are told it will avail
them nothing, with Job, who is commanded to scuff the ground
and obeys, so his hurt is lifted/removed by the water of the
spring. It tells of the touch of *pain* that may come from God to
the evildoers, thereby highlighting the paradox that Satan can
touch Job with *hardship and pain* and that *hurt* can touch him.
The punishment is so terrible that "The unbelievers if touched
by a breath of God's punishment cry out, but there will be
no relief for them." It tells that Muhammad warns them by an
inspiration given to him, albeit they are deaf to his warning
(v. 45): "Yet if even a breath of the Lord's punishment were
to touch them, they would say 'Woe are we, indeed we have
been sinners'" (v. 46). Harm touches Job; he is put to the test
by what is evil, yet he calls out and is saved.

## III

The pericope from al-An'am may be rendered as follows:

> 83 Thus was Our argument
> We gave it to Abraham to convince his people.
> We raise in rank whom We will
> —Your Lord is indeed Wise, Knowing.
> 84 We gave to him Isaac and Jacob,
> each of them We guided.
> And before them We guided Noah,
> and of his posterity We guided
> David, Solomon, Job,
> Joseph, Moses and Aaron
> —thus We reward those who do good—
> 85 together with Zachariya and John, Jesus and Elias,

—each of them was one of the righteous—
86 and Ismail and Elisha, Jonah and Lot
—each of them We favoured above all others—
87 and of their forebears and posterity and brethren
—We chose them and guided them to a straight path.
88 Thus is the guidance of God
He guides with it whom of His servants He wills
Yet were they to put aught beside Him,
all they have done would fall from them.
89 It is these to whom We have given
the Book, Wisdom and Prophecy
yet if these were to disbelieve in it,
then We would give it to a people who would not be
    faithless to it.
90 It is these whom God has guided,
So [Muhammad] follow the guidance given them.

Here too, Job is included in an assembly of prophets, although after Jacob the chronology is structured to emphasize their commonality and community, showing Job as a member of this community, with his own place and charism. The pericope is addressed to Muhammad. From one standpoint its words are of comfort and support addressed to him, telling him that just as these were prophets, so is he. But equally important, it is a hymnodic celebration of God's providence. It celebrates God for his wisdom in choosing them—"Your Lord is indeed Wise and Knowing." It tells of the guidance and blessing given to them, their kin and their families—"thus do We reward those who do good." It emphasizes their virtues—"each of them was of the righteous," and how they had been raised to a rank above all other humankind—"each of them We favored above all

others." It gives the reminder, however, that if they had failed
to lived up to their calling and the guidance they had been
given, they would be as nothing. Muhammad is urged to follow the guidance given them. This guidance is given to each
according to his situation and needs. In the case of Abraham it
had been for the argument to confront his father and his kin.
In the case of Job, it was in relation to his particular trial, to
call to God as the Merciful.

## IV

The fourth pericope, al-Nisa' (4, vv. 163–165), may be rendered as follows:

> 163 We have made a revelation to you as We made it
> to Noah and those succeeding him,
> and we made it to Abraham, Ishmael, Isaac, Jacob
> and his descendants Jesus, Job,
> Jonah, Aaron, and Solomon,
> —to David We gave the psalms!—
> 164 and to messengers We have told you of previously,
> and to messengers of whom We have not told you
> —to Moses God spoke directly!—
> 165 messengers giving good tiding and warning
> that humankind might have no claim (hujja) against
>     God
> once messengers [had been sent them],
> God being mighty and wise.

Here again, Job has a place among an assembly of prophets
largely coinciding with those named in the other pericopes,

but extended to include prophets of whom Muhammad has
not been told, a phrase that adds a universalistic dimension
to the pericope. These prophets are presented as messengers
giving good tidings and warning without reference to any of
their words or deeds. There are no laudatory formulae, they are
presented solely as recipients of revelation. The sura now under
consideration, however, is a Madinan sura, so plays an important
role as a source for the bases and principles of Islamic law, in
particular family law and the position, rights, and responsibili-
ties of women. Nevertheless, it resounds with the great themes
of the Islamic revelation epitomized in a verse such as "God,
there is no God but He! Most surely He will assemble you on
the Day of Resurrection, there is no doubt of it" (v. 87). Indeed,
alongside its legal provisions, the sura offers a kaleidoscope of
doxology, prophetology, and theodicy. There are, however, two
verses that give a special place to Abraham, and as such relate
directly to the pericope under discussion, and through it to the
Abraham scene presented in al-An'am and the guidance passed
on to Job. The first is "For We gave the descendants of Abraham
the Book and Wisdom, and We gave them a mighty kingdom"
(v. 54). The second is, "Who is better as to his religion than
one who submits his face (*wajhahu*) to God, he being one who
follows the religion of Abraham in total sincerity (*hanifan*) [or
as a *hanif*]. God took Abraham as a friend" (v. 125). The first
establishes the position of Abraham and prepares the way for
the naming of some of his prophetic progeny in this pericope.
The second, by its reference to "one who turns his face (*wajhahu*) to God," and "who follows the religion of Abraham . . ."
(*hanifan*), by the placing of the words *wajhahu* and *hanifan* in
close proximity here, trigger in the mind an association with

Abraham's profession of faith: "I indeed, I turn my face to Him who created the heavens and the earth in total sincerity (*'ani-fan*)" (6:79), after God had given him his *argument* by showing him the setting of star, moon, and sun (6:76–78). Yet there is another thread to the skein. The wonderful phrase *God took Abraham as a friend* has a direct association with the phrase in the pericope *to Moses God spoke directly* (v. 164). These two prophets have titles that distinguish them above all others: Moses is Kalim Allah, "the man with whom God spoke," and Abraham is Khalil Allah, "God's friend." So the inclusion of Job in this sura reinforces the intimacy between the Creator and the prophet Job.

## Conclusion

While the Qur'an presents Job as a lesser prophet, in the sense explained, we have tried to show something of the vitality and moral passion concentrated in so few verses. Each of the four pericopes in which he occurs either contributes information about him or reveals a perspective of his position within the community of prophets, and his relation to the prophetic experience of Muhammad. Viewed synoptically, they provide a model in miniature of the rhetorical genius of the Qur'an, especially when illumined by the intertextualities within them uncovered by Tabari in his exegesis of the Job episode in al-Anbiya'. A closer reading, however, immediately involves the student in the broader context to which these attestations of Job belong. For it then becomes clear that his profile as a prophet is achieved not simply because he is an individual referred to only four times, but by the way he is integrated into the community of prophets, individuals various in their vocations and styles, but sharing a common vocation and a common reward. As a result, the richness of their vocation, and the varying emphases of the divine messages given them, is revealed, and the account they give of themselves shows and justifies Muhammad's role and vocation. For the prophets complement each other, and references to and narratives about them establish an echoing grove in which the distinctive features of Job's prophetic charism are highlighted and brought into focus.

We have shown how the pericopes themselves display Job and his prophet companions from varying perspectives, emphasizing different themes. In the Sad pericope a leading theme is that belief is a prior condition for a call to God to be answered. Thus, Solomon first asked pardon for a fault and then asked God for a kingdom such as that possessed by none other, addressing him as *al-Wahhab*, The Bestower. He was given power of the winds and the demons (38:35–38). Job called for relief from hardship and pain. His call was likewise answered, and God gave back to him the kin that had been taken from him, and restored his health (38:41–43). But when the time came for the unbelievers who rejected the Prophet to call for relief when their punishment was about to overwhelm them, their call would be in vain (38:3). In al-Anbiya' a dominant theme is of God being true to his word to his prophets, hearing them when they call, saving them from physical danger, removing from them oppression, and bestowing on them what they ask. In al-An'am emphasis is on the argument that God gives to his prophets to enable them to answer those who reject his message, and the assurance that they will be guided to the argument (*hujja*) that they need. In al-Nisa' a predominant theme is the continuity and consistency of God's sending messengers to numbers of peoples, some of them known, some unknown, to numerous communities to ensure that his will is known, and that accordingly, humankind cannot claim ignorance as an excuse for their sinfulness.

All four pericopes are interrelated acoustically, conceptually, and thematically, often concentrating the essence of a wide range of associations in a single word, which if "leaned on," discloses a richness and diversity of meanings at a number of levels. In each, Job is shown from a different perspective, one that throws an individual light both on himself and on the prophets with whom he is associated, in accordance with the character of the pericope. Thus, in Sad he is placed with David and Solomon at the core of a symmetrically structured pericope. The difference between him and them (David and Solomon are prophet kings) draws attention to the special character of his prophetic vocation, as one who suffers and whose message is preached by his endurance of undeserved suffering. God says of him, "Indeed We found him patient" (38:44). As such he is presented as a role model for Muhammad in the face of rejection, to whom God says, "Be patient in face of what they say" (38:17). In al-Anbiya', among a more extended panorama of prophets, he is associated in particular with two of them, Jonah and Zechariah, whose calls to God, like his, are given in direct speech. All three are in torment, but for different reasons: Job because of the hurt that is upon him (loss of family and the pain of disease), Jonah in the darkness of the whale after his outburst of anger, and Zechariah in anguish at his childlessness. Each of them addresses God in his own way. Job calls on him as "Most merciful of the merciful"; Jonah calls on him in a formula of recognition and praise, "There is no God but You. Glory to You!"; and Zechariah calls on him as "Best of inheritors." God answers each of them. The hurt is taken from Job, Jonah is saved from the darkness that oppresses him, and Zechariah is given a son. As in Sad, Job is one of a core group of three prophets that forms a focus of tension in the pericope dominated by Abraham's rejection of all gods but God, Abraham the very model of those rescued from danger when God saved him from the fire (21:69).

In al-An'am, Job's inclusion in the assembly of the prophets, in addition to his place among those to whom God has given guidance, serves as a reminder that just as Muhammad suffered one kind of hurt because those to whom he preached the Qur'an rejected him, so too did one of his predecessors, Job, a brother prophet, who was touched by hurt (*durr*), and whom Satan had touched with hardship and pain. Yet without complaint he called to the "Most merciful of the merciful." In al-Nisa', Job is included in a celebratory concourse of prophets eulogizing God's providence in the sending of prophets. It is marked by a striking reversal of context in the use of the word *hujja* [argument]. God sent the prophets so that man may have no *argument* against God. And this is sufficient to trigger a memory of the *argument* that God gave to Abraham (6:83) that no human opponent could refute.

Together these four pericopes show Job as a member of the community of prophets with a distinctive place and a special charism: that he should suffer without knowing why, and instead of despairing, cry to God for relief, trusting in God as the Merciful. This is what makes him, and God's answer to him, a lesson "to those with understanding" (38:43). This discussion has barely touched the surface of the richness, complexities, and shared intertextualities within these four pericopes. It is sufficient, however, to show how elaborate is the intertext sustained and informed by the exegetic tradition, and the network of themes and verbal echoes that are one aspect of the unity of the Qur'an. They yield spiritual meanings and disclose some of the aspects of the literary dimension of the Qur'an once the relevant reference points that point to its internal structure have been discovered. It may therefore bring to light hitherto unexplored aspects of the literary and religious dynamics of the Qur'an. It has also drawn attention to some of the ways in which the Qur'an as divine revelation plays its role in the religious life and imagination of the Muslim world. It prompts reflection on the varying responses to revelation in different, albeit related, religious traditions. Divine revelation presents an image of a spiritual rhythm that both clashes and harmonizes with the human rhythms of everyday life. In the Western tradition memories of the exemplars by which this divine rhythm is carried are presented visually through a complex iconography that serves as an emotional trigger to activate, and so realize, these rhythms. In the Islamic tradition, however, which largely rejects the role of visual images, such emotional triggers are provided by the language of the Qur'an, which in its own way presents vivid verbal images of natural phenomena, of heaven and hell, of the confrontation of good and evil, and the human situation in general, without the need to depict the physical characteristics of any individual. It is the language itself that constitutes the iconic tradition. Not a single word can be taken or heard in isolation. All represent nuclei of meaning that are cumulative and that cohere, serving as triggers to activate the profoundest depths of religious consciousness.[4]

As a counterpoint to our already wide-ranging theological reflection on the biblical book of Job, Anthony Johns's careful reading of the Qur'anic texts has shown us how the figure of Job enunciates and intensifies standing themes of Qur'anic revelation. And while the Qur'anic presentation of Job cannot be said to have the corrective point that distinguishes the extended biblical poem, we have been able to glimpse something of the genius of that book's composition through a sophisticated reading (albeit sketchy) of those portions devoted to this prophet. Moreover, readers following Anthony Johns's manner of delineating the figure of Job will have learned some of the skills required to attain a penetrating reading of the Qur'an itself.

4. These ideas are suggested by a paragraph in *History of Italian Art, Volume Two,* Claire Dory, trans. (Oxford: Polity Press, 1994), 129, brought to my attention by Dr. A. D. Street.

# 6

# CLASSICAL
# COMMENTARIES

*Saadiah, Maimonides, Aquinas, and Gersonides*

THE VERY VENTURE of a "theological reflection" harks back to medieval times, where the book of Job inspired extended theological reflections, first by Saadiah Gaon (882–942), and then by Moses ben Maimon [Maimonides] (1135–1204), Thomas Aquinas (1225–1274), and Levi ben Gershom [Gersonides] (1288–1344), in Jewish and Christian traditions; while the previous chapter offers insightful reflections on the brief Qur'anic treatment of the figure of Ayyub [Job]. It may at first appear startling that there is so little congruence among these readings, yet a little reflection would show that poetry invites a welter of readings, as does this topic of the creator God and human suffering, whose resolution (were it posed as a "problem") would defy rational measure.

## Saadiah

The earliest of these commentaries, by Saadiah ben Joseph (known as Saadiah Gaon from his role leading the longstanding Talmudic academy of Sura in Babylon), was composed in an Islamic intellectual environment that moved Saadiah to render the book of Job into Arabic, as well as to compose his commentary in that dominant language. We are admirably served by Lenn Goodman's translation of text and commentary into English, with an extended introduction (plus ample explanatory notes to the text and commentary) locating Saadiah's preoccupations within the Islamic commentary tradition on the figure of Job, notably the patterns prevailing among the Mu'tazilite exegesis exemplified by al-Zamakhshari (d. 1143) (Goodman 1988). Distinguishing among four ways of presenting the figure of Job—"metaphysical, exemplary, figural and fabular" (34)—Goodman has this to say about the "metaphysical" mode:

> The metaphysical reading of the Book of Job, which develops as an integrated topos in the theological writings of Saadiah, to be carried further by Maimonides and Gersonides, is focused with the aid of Mu'tazilite grammatical exegesis, dialogic methods, critical standards, and theological concerns—specifically in theodicy. This focus is actively preserved from dissolution or distraction into quite a variety of tangential interests, which are . . . more than amply represented in the Midrash and *Tafsir* (58).

In this vein, Saadiah sees suffering as (1) for the sake of discipline and instruction (2) purgation and punishment, or (3) trial and testing (125). Saadiah sees Job's suffering as a trial, noting that were God to have assured him of a salutary outcome, it could hardly have been a trial. Goodman identifies this move as the kernel of the book's theodicy, as Saadiah unveils it:

> It is a central thesis of Saadiah's theological commentary that Job's sufferings were undeserved, just as the Book of Job maintains. Despite God's justice, misfortune does not imply guilt. Saadiah maintains that suffering, when undeserved, has a meaning and a purpose in God's plan for Israel and for the world and nature at large. To sustain this claim, Saadiah, like the Book of Job itself, must lean out beyond the comforting assurances of the Mosaic and prophetic ideas of the covenantal promises, and risk departure from the most familiar interpretations of the Biblical prophets and Rabbinic sages, to discover the larger cosmological meaning of the Mosaic idea of God's covenant with nature. His purpose is to vindicate the central thesis of God's justice in and through nature (94).

Goodman summarizes Saadiah's synthetic comment on the voice from the whirlwind:

> The three themes elicited by Saadiah from the torrent of symbols loosed in Job's mind by the raging of the storm are . . . the act of creation, the constitution of the order and powers of nature, and the providential governance by which nature is overseen. . . . Uniting these three themes is the single concept which Saadiah identifies as that of God's sovereignty over nature, providing chastisements and rewards but also trials. For the creatures who undergo them the meaning of such trials is

inevitably problematic. Indeed they are discernable as trials
only to the self-governed and self-knowing heart. Their ultimate purposiveness will not be divulged by an external source
of knowledge, not even by divine speech [lest they cease to
be trials]. Even so, if we give up the expectation of a kind of
certainty incommensurate with our humanity, we can discern
a character uniting all the aspects of God's active sovereignty.
The message which Saadiah finds Job to have discerned pro-
phetically in the tenor of God's governance is that of grace,
the theme with which his commentary opens [in the form of
a prefatory blessing] (99–100):

Blessed be the Lord, God of Israel, eternal before all things
that begin, everlasting beyond all things that end, Creator and
Originator, who sets our term and will restore us, to whom
praise and thanksgiving are due for His universal grace and
all-encompassing beneficence (123).

We shall see (chapter 7) how closely this theodicy hews to
Marilyn McCord Adams's sense of *resources* available to believers, rather than to any purported "explanation" of undeserved
suffering. Saadiah can find restorative themes in God's enig-
matic response without ever attempting to remove the enigma.
For our purposes, Saadiah's commentary sets the stage for the
later medieval "metaphysical" efforts of Maimonides, Aquinas,
and Gersonides, yet Goodman's competence in exposing the
Islamic context within which he composed it reveals the richness of a commentary which on the face of it could appear
rather pedestrian. He also helps us move forward by deftly
responding to potential objectors in exposing the reasons for
his fascination with Saadiah:

It may be protested that the metaphysical approach to Job developed by Maimonides and Gersonides from the insights which Saadiah had put forward at the stimulus of his philosophic readings and his contact with the *Kalam* and the Mu'tazilite theodicy and methodic are no more than rationales, that the Biblical text eludes philosophy, surpassing or failing to reach the level of discourse employed by Maimonides and his ilk, that rationale is rationalization, and that only tradition can encompass the authentic meaning of Scripture. Examination of the materials preserved within the nonconceptually oriented Midrash and *Tafsir* provides ample evidence (as with the conceptual material) of intercultural cross-pollination and the fertility of the Midrashic method as a means of elaboration. Curiously enough, it also bears even more striking evidence of the inadequacy of the methods of tradition and traditionalism in the maintenance and development of any sort of coherent thematic (62–63).

This "theological reflection" need not proffer so overt a justification for selecting these authors to elucidate scripture, yet it is worth recording Goodman's *apologia* for the delicate balance it evidences. Moreover, our journey thus far could lead us to affirm as well that "the Biblical text eludes philosophy," in the sense that the book of Job will effectively challenge those philosophical forays into these tangled issues which overlook the ineffable relation between creator and creatures. Indeed, the way in which Saadiah highlights the theme of creation as central to his account of the import of the book of Job affords the most salient reason, as we shall see, for privileging his commentary.

## Maimonides, Aquinas, and Gersonides[1]

The book of Job remains the classic religious document to criticize inadequate accounts believers might offer for their God's conduct. There is no comparable document in Islam, for the simple reason (I suspect) that Job presses to its limits a practice that the Bible countenanced as early as Abraham yet which is nowhere licensed in the Qur'an: argument with the Holy One. We have used the work of Anthony Johns, however, to cast some comparative light on the figure of Job [Ayyub] in the Qur'an, to explore the role he plays. In Jewish tradition, Moses ben Maimonides and Levi ben Gersonides both treat the book of Job as a proto-philosophical treatise, finding each interlocutor espousing positions known to them historically, yet also neatly representing available logical alternatives. In their resolutions, Maimonides sides with the Torah—"that the various events are known to God before they take place [but that such] knowledge of one of two eventualities does not determine it" (*Guide* 3.2)—while Gersonides stands with "philosophic thought," leaving God ignorant of what will happen except as "ordered and defined" (*Wars of Lord* 3.4). So the problematic shifts from the person of Job and his affliction to the modalities of God's acting in God's world. Yet with their Muslim conversation partners, neither attends to human freedom except as a check on divine omnipotence.

Aquinas is positioned historically between his Jewish colleagues yet partakes in a tradition more practiced in grammatical reflections. These allow him to reconcile a respect for

1. Some of the following has been excerpted from David Burrell, "Maimonides, Aquinas and Gersonides on Providence and Evil," *Religious Studies* 20 (1984): 335–51.

scripture and divine transcendence with the demands of logic, while directing him to locate the difficulty we have in articulating God's knowledge of particulars with the fact that "we cannot speak of divine knowing except in our mode of understanding, using tensed discourse," whereas "divine knowing is measured by eternity" (*Q. D. de Veritate* [*Disputed Questions on Truth*] 2.12). So "God knows contingent things as each one of them is itself in act" (*Summa Theologiae* [=*ST*] 1.14.13). Such is the grammar of the matter, which demands closer analysis, for it apparently asserts that what (in time) will happen is the same as what (in eternity) is happening. But we shall see how such recondite metaphysical issues can indeed be employed to lend credence to our rendition of the book of Job.

In presenting these three characters I shall respond more to systematic concerns than to chronology. For while Maimonides stands in the twelfth century, Aquinas in the thirteenth, and Gersonides in the fourteenth, the communication networks so functioned as to put Gersonides into closer contact with Maimonides than with Aquinas. There were cultural and linguistic reasons for this proximity: it is questionable, for example, whether Gersonides read Latin, even though he lived in Provence. Moreover, given the links of Jewish learning with Muslim Spain, he appears to be more beholden to Averroes than to Western scholastics. It is perhaps the influence of Averroes— that highly systematic thinker whom the West called simply "the Commentator," to acknowledge his fidelity to Aristotle— that gives to Gersonides's writing that directness and clarity one associates with the early scholastics. In this respect he can certainly be said to have assimilated the thought patterns of his time. Yet for all that, as we shall see, his philosophic *mode*

remains beholden to that thought world which he shares with
Maimonides, and from which Aquinas learned but to which he
remained an outsider, Islamic philosophy. In another respect,
however, Maimonides and Aquinas are closer to each another
in spirit than Gersonides is to either, in their respect for the
life of the faith community as a factor in theological reflection.
In this respect Gersonides offers a more purely philosophical
interpretation of the issues than they do, and in so doing gives
inadvertent testimony to Islamic positions on these vexing
questions.

What is fascinating is that each specifically comments on
the book of Job. And if the two relatively short chapters that
Maimonides contributes in *The Guide for the Perplexed* cannot rightly be called a commentary, they nonetheless inspired
Gersonides to compose his quite extensive work, for he found
Maimonides's reflections to be the only sensible thing he had
been able to turn up on that "strange and wonderful book"
(Maimonides 1956, 3.22–23). Moreover, Maimonides's manner of reading the book shaped Levi ben Gershom's, for each
assigns distinct philosophical positions to Job's friends, and each
assimilates the argument of Elihu, the last interlocutor, to his
own (Levi ben Gershom 1946). Aquinas proves more sensitive
to the literary genre of the work, often pausing to remark on its
poetic features (Aquinas 1965). He is drawn in this direction
because he expressly proposes a literal treatment of the work,
thereby breaking from the pattern of allegorical interpretation
of Job fashioned by Gregory. Maimonides also remarks that it
is a "great poem" (3.22), but in offering his "explanation" of it
treats it as a philosophical treatise.

The positions that Maimonides and Gersonides associate with each of Job's friends are more important for what they reveal of these thinkers' respective preoccupations than for what they assert. Maimonides divides the house among Torah believers holding human beings to a strict justice, since they are invariably the cause of all evil befalling them (Eliphaz); the Ash'arites, who hold that divine will causes everything (Zophar); and the Mu'tazilites, who must contrive a recompense for every action, good or evil (Bildad) (3.23). Gersonides finds these latter two positions unworthy of philosophic consideration and finds a logical way of assigning the three roles. If one queries, in sympathy with Job, why the just should suffer and the evil prosper, there are three plausible ways of dealing with the complaint. One can admit it and locate responsibility with men (Eliphaz), or one can contest the complaint: on the part of the subject—they are not really just/evil (Zophar), or of the predicate—they are not really suffering/prospering (Bildad). And, he tries to argue in all fairness, each response can be presented quite plausibly. Yet not quite, of course, as the narrative shows.

What proves disappointing, however, is that Gersonides makes no effort to show why he can call Elihu's position his own. By this time he seems to have lost interest in the dialogue, and his position, as we shall see, does not bear any relation to it. And Maimonides's explanation for Elihu's superiority turns on an obscure interpretation of a passing reference to the intercession of an angel. What is far more interesting, in fact, are the different attitudes that Maimonides and Aquinas assume toward Job himself (who plays no defined role in Gersonides's presentation.) Maimonides turns his fierce complaints into an ideology, identifying him with Aristotle, for whom there in effect is no special providence for individuals. The denouement of the drama then becomes "the Revelation that reached Job and explained to him the error of his whole belief" (3.23). God's commendation (Job 42:7) then envisages the Job who was converted. And this was accomplished only when "he had acquired a true knowledge of God." In fact, "so long as Job's knowledge of God was based on tradition and communication, and not on research (= by the way of speculation [Pines]), he believed that such imaginary good as is possessed in health, riches and children was the utmost that men can attain" (3.23).

For Aquinas, the situation is exactly the opposite. Job is the just man par excellence, and it is his friends who constantly confuse temporal goods with beatitude, thinking at once that Job *must* have done evil since *everything* has been taken away from him. Aquinas pictures Job as exercised, indeed, that his lot has so radically changed, yet possessed of an unerring sense for what one may and may not say about God's ways with us, for his heart is focused on the true good, God, and his mind is clear about his eternal destiny. Vociferous as his complaint is, he never wavers in essentials, and so is deserving of God's commendation—indeed of God's response. Job's own retraction (Job 42:6), says Aquinas, repents rather of the *way* he has spoken, in that it could have given scandal, or may reflect such a keen appreciation of God's justice that he recognizes how far he is from the mark—much as saints can genuinely call themselves sinners (212, 218).

In the end, I am afraid that the fact of these commentaries is more significant than their impact on the thinking of any of our protagonists, all of whom more or less evacuate the dramatic impact of the poem by assimilating it to a treatise. Maimonides's attempt to identify the remonstrations of Job's friends with diverse philosophical positions defies the most discerning reading of the text. In this respect Aquinas is the more faithful reader, since he never finds them making more than minor variations on the same tired ideology. In the measure that Gersonides's followed the lead of his predecessor, he too mislocates the dramatic center. Aquinas will identify it accurately—in the contrast between the "hymn to wisdom" (Job 28) and the Lord's actual address (Job 38:34): "since human wishes will prove insufficient to comprehend the truth of divine providence, it was necessary that this dispute be determined by divine authority" (199). It is the actual speaking— God's responding to Job—that offers the dramatic point of the poem: the determination by divine authority. Yet Aquinas does not exploit this "performative" dimension, assured as he is (from the earlier "hymn to wisdom") that "wisdom can attune us to the *ratio* of divine providence: that spiritual goods are given to the just as the better [reward], while temporal goods may go to the unjust, but these are of course quite worthless (*caduca*)" (155)!

And in this wisdom-teaching they all, as we might expect, concur. Moreover, some such orientation will certainly be present in any theological treatment of this classic complaint, yet one would have hoped for a clearer recognition that the "spiritual goods" in question really amount to a personal relationship between the one so vigorously complaining and the Lord of the universe—a relationship effected by that One's actual response to the plaintiff. That is how one could exploit the *performative* character of the poem. Maimonides and Gersonides are kept from doing this by their deliberate recasting of it as a treatise, Aquinas by his insistence on Job's holiness throughout and by locating that primarily (if not principally) in his right *belief* about immorality. For since that teaching is already available to wisdom (philosophy), the confirmation that God's response brings is prevented from adding anything substantive to the argument.

## A Cumulative Shift to God's Mode of Knowing

Maimonides will read the sense of the Lord's response, which "describes the elements, meteorological phenomena, and peculiarities of various kinds of living beings," as serving "to impress on our minds that we are unable to comprehend how these transient creatures come into existence . . . and that these are not like the things which we are able to produce. Much less can we compare the manner in which God rules and manages his creatures with the manner in which we rule and manage certain things" (3.23). To be sure, this "lesson [that he takes to be] the principal object of the whole book of Job" concurs with Maimonides's way of resolving the dilemmas that arise when we simultaneously affirm God's foreknowledge and responsible human freedom; yet it also comes close *as a reading* to incorporating the drama of the poem: what is most significant is not *what* God says, but the impact on us of God's saying it. Namely, that "we should not fall into the error of imagining His knowledge to be similar to ours, or His intention, providence, and rule similar to ours" (3.23).

Yet Rabbi Moses (as Aquinas always called him) had already arrived at that place, and this time it is Gersonides who will show how unstable a position it is. All three of them will affirm with Isaiah, certainly: "as the heavens are higher than the earth, so my ways are higher than your ways" (Isa. 55:9), yet neither Aquinas nor Gersonides will want to conclude therefrom that "our knowledge . . . has only the name in common with God's knowledge" (3.20). In fact, Gersonides judges that his predecessor's notorious agnosticism regarding divine attributes actually stems from this specific impasse (Samuelson 1977, 130–39; 1976, 71–82). For Maimonides accepts "that God's knowledge extends to things not in existence . . . but the existence of which God foresees and is able to effect." Yet he also insists that "according to the teaching of our law, God's knowledge of one of two eventualities does not determine it, however certain that knowledge may be concerning the future occurrence of the one eventuality" (3.20). For if it did, human choice would be rendered otiose, and the entire structure of the covenant "set[ting] before you life and prosperity, death and disaster" (Deut. 30:15) would collapse. So Maimonides must conclude that "as we cannot accurately comprehend His essence, and yet we know that His existence is most perfect, . . . so we have no correct notion of His knowledge, because it is nothing but His essence, and yet we are convinced that . . . He obtains no new knowledge . . . and [that] nothing of all existing things escapes His knowledge, but their nature is not changed thereby; that which is possible remains possible" (3.20).

As we shall see, all the assertions are in place for a resolution uncannily similar to that which Aquinas will propose, with the one crucial difference that Maimonides fails to factor in the decisive relation of time to eternity. By letting the locution go by uncriticized—"that the various events are known to Him *before* they take place" (3.20)—Maimonides misses an opportunity radically to qualify the comparison of God's knowledge to ours, and must move to the yet more radical denial of any comparison whatsoever. Yet, as Gersonides will show clearly, that is more than a radical move; it is a self-defeating act of desperation. For if one were to carry it out, one would be prevented from using any reference to God's knowing in an argument. And since Maimonides's treatment of providence (in the preceding chapter) did appeal to such knowledge to argue that nothing actuated by the Creator should be concealed from him, Gersonides's critique finds its mark (Samuelson 1977, 124–39).

Before leaving Maimonides to consider Gersonides's constructive alternative, we should attend to an earlier chapter where he criticizes inquiries into "the purpose of creation" (3.13). Taking his lead from Ibn-Sina [Avicenna], he reminds us that "a final cause must exist for everything that owes its existence to an intelligent being: but for that which is without a beginning, a final cause need not be sought" (3.13).[2] Whether one argues from creation or from the eternity of the universe, "there is no occasion to seek the final cause of the whole Universe," since its originator does not act according to a purpose. The most we can say is that "each [species-] being exists for its own sake" and that "each part [of the universe] is . . . the product of God's will"; in short, that "God saw that it was good" (Gen.1:4). There is then no sense in trying to ascertain God's *intentions* in creating and guiding the universe as a whole, that is, in the order among its

---

2. The background for this axiom can be found in Etienne Gilson's classical article: "Pourquoi St. Thomas a critiqué St. Augustin," *Archives d'histoire doctrinale et littéraire du Moyen Age* I (Paris: Vrin, 1926–27).

parts, since that order is not susceptible of functional language, which would be our way of explaining it.

We should continue to affirm and to admire the existence of a divine order—indeed we must presume *order* in any inquiry—and pondering it allows us to "obtain a correct estimation of ourselves" (3.14). Such, we recall, was his way of taking the Lord's response to Job. Yet we are not thereby licensed to construct a functional explanation—say of a "higher good" resulting from this disaster or that—in fact, we are effectively blocked from doing just that. What I find so fascinating about this chapter is not only its astute conclusion, but also the fact that we can watch Maimonides engage in a discerning discrimination between God's knowing and ours, and do so with philosophical acumen and religious sensitivity. Moreover, this chapter contains the germs of a criticism of Gersonides's position quite as trenchant as the way his successor logically dismantles Maimonides. Even more trenchant, in fact, for these observations call into question the properly *explanatory* value of any emanation scheme purporting to relate God to the universe.

Yet that is exactly what Levi ben Gershom will propose, and try to align with the Torah as well. He will do so by arranging the alternatives as his philosophical context allows him to do, and opposing himself not only to Maimonides's self-defeating conclusion, but also to his stated features of divine knowing—what we might call the givens of the Jewish tradition. Asking the generic question whether God knows contingent particulars, he divides the house between "the Philosopher and his followers" and "the great sages of the Torah" (Samuelson 1977, 101, 98). The sages, including Maimonides, insist that God knows "contingent particulars as particulars" (101), while those followers of

Aristotle whom he chooses to treat admit that "he only knows himself" yet argue that "in his knowledge of himself he knows everything that exists insofar as it possesses a universal nature. The reason for this is that he is the *nomos*, the order and the arrangement [*nimus, seder, yoser*] of existing beings." This second position, indistinguishable from Ibn-Sina's, will become that of Gersonides as well. Yet he must first show how the position of the sages, best displayed in Maimonides, is incoherent, while his own scheme answers to the very concerns of the tradition that their assertions intended to convey. This will be difficult, for Gersonides—never one to conceal an implication, however unwelcome—warns us that on this position God "does not know particulars" (100).

The ploy is not a difficult one for philosophers, of course, who need only to show that such knowledge does not constitute a perfection, so that God's lacking it will not amount to a deprivation in divinity. Yet such an argument will sound very odd in a tradition that produced the book of Job. Gersonides has a general principle for dealing with that oddness, however, and its formulations appear to come directly from Ibn Rushd [Averroes] *Kitab fasl al-Maqal*: "whenever the Torah, according to what appears from the external meaning of its words, disagrees with some things which are clear from the point of view of Philosophic Thought, it is proper that we should interpret them in a manner which is in agreement with Philosophic Thought" (Samuelson 1977, 300–301 n. 620). He claims, moreover, that this principle adequately formulates Maimonides's stated intent and normal practice in the *Guide*, so that deviations have to be seen as contradicting his own principles (302). Yet it is doubtful whether the text from the introductory letter to Joseph Ibn Aknin will stand so unilateral a reading, and the most fruitful principles of interpretation allow actual practice to determine the sense of a criterion offered (303–6 n. 621). Yet Gersonides must call his predecessor's practice into question to justify his own.

The rest is quite routine, following directly from God as defined to be "the *nomos*, the order and the arrangement of existing things" (100). So we can say that God knows particulars, though not as particulars; God knows them in "the respect in which they are ordered and defined" (232 n. 345). (For a more extensive treatment, see Samuelson 1972.) The rest of his treatment amounts to saying this in different ways, which testify to its source yet offer little clarification: "in knowing things as emanating from His essence, God knows their intelligible orderings" (244), for God knows the "orderings from which these acts [of creating] emanate, and which are performed instrumentally by Active Intellect and the heavenly bodies" (239–40). In the fourth book of *The Wars of the Lord*, he will go into greater detail concerning the role the spheres play in guiding those attuned to them toward the good and away from misfortune (Touati 1968, 133–35, 149–50). Yet what becomes essential there is not God's care, but our aligning ourselves with that order so as to receive its benefits. The theory of prophecy familiar from al-Farabi and Ibn-Sina becomes his way of tapping into divine providence. And as for the order that particulars do have, it "is just ultimately and a good ordering" (257). The end of the argument—and of all argument!

Before moving to Aquinas, we should consider a dimension of Gersonides's responses to Maimonides in which he appears to utilize that special form of equivocation that Aquinas developed as *analogy*. In fact, he asserts that there is a particular fashion in which God's knowledge is equivocal with ours: "by priority and posteriority" (186). This is the famous *per prius et posterius* of Aquinas, and his manner of elaborating it reminds one of Aquinas's adopting the neoplatonic scheme: *per essentiam/ per participationem:* like "'knowledge,' 'existent,' 'one,' 'entity' . . . are said of God priorly and of other beings posteriorly . . . because His existence, His oneness, and His entity belong to Him essentially, and from Him emanate the existence, the oneness and the entity of every existing thing" (186–87). Yet when he puts the scheme to work, the real differences among things, which analogy was crafted to handle, disappear: "there is no difference between the knowledge of God . . . and our knowledge except that the knowledge of God . . . is more perfect than our knowledge" (188). Just what Maimonides feared: the distance between creator and creature becomes one of degree. And feared wisely, for Gersonides's conversation partners were the same as his, and the clarity which they sought from philosophy would be purchased by an unalterable faith in single stratum of meaning underlying the various uses of a term: "the distance in meaning between these predicates and those like them, when they are said of Him . . . is like the distance between His level of existence . . . and their level of existence in terms of the perfection and excellence of being. I mean to say that they are said in a more perfect way of God . . . than the way in which they are said of what is other than Him" (223–24.). He has said enough, certainly, to realize that he thinks there to be something common to all things, something called *being*, which is realized essentially in God and in which creatures participate. There is some evidence that this

does represent Ibn-Sina's position, and even better evidence
that it was never Aquinas's (Gardet 1951; Burrell 1963).

So the very feature of Gersonides's thought that brings him
closest to the scholastic tradition in the West shows him rather
beholden to the scheme of intelligible emanation that Ibrahim
Madkour celebrates as the specific contribution of Arab philosophy (Madkour 1934, 14). What I find to criticize in such
a pattern is not its source—the medievals can teach us all a
lesson in accepting truth wherever it is to be found. What
this preoccupation with order and definition in characterizing
God's knowledge leads us to overlook, however, is precisely
the master image associated with a creation story: that of the
craftsman. Gersonides cites this expression but uses it only to
show how "the heavenly bodies are His instruments" (227),
and he soon transmutes it into that of "an architect of a house
[who] should know the form of the bricks and the beams"
(230). So in the end his description is of speculative knowing, even if the image the tradition offers insists on an active,
working knowledge.

Maimomides explicitly invokes the image of an artisan to
show what "a great difference [there is] between the knowledge
which the producer of a thing possesses concerning it, and the
knowledge which other persons possess concerning the same
thing" (3.21). He even goes on to note how every object is du-
ally related: "to our knowledge and [to] God's knowledge of it"
(3:21). "His knowledge of things is not derived from the things
themselves; . . . on the contrary, the things are in accordance
with His eternal knowledge." Now, "this kind of knowledge
cannot be comprehended by us" certainly, as he insists, yet
one would also agree with him "that this is an excellent idea,

and leads to correct views" (3.21). But what more is an analogy supposed to do than what Maimonides has done with this
one (Burrell 1992)? I shall follow his lead, in expounding and
developing Aquinas's use of this same image, incorporating as
well the factor that Maimonides overlooked: the model, proper
to divinity, of eternity.

For Aquinas too accepts as his controlling axiom that God's
knowledge relates to things not as derived from them but as
causing them (*Summa Theologiae* [=*ST*] 1.14.8). Moreover,
such knowledge extends not only to forms but to matter. For
without being able to say *how* this is so, we know that if God
knows things other than himself in his essence, then his essence
must comprehend whatever comes into existence through
him—and not merely in their universal natures but in their
individuality. In this central argument Aquinas warns us not to
limit God's knowing by specious comparisons with our own. For
the original contrast between our knowing and God's already
suggests a powerful image: "natural things are [suspended]
between God's knowledge and ours, for we receive ours from
those very things which God causes through his knowledge"
(*ST* 1.14.8.3) (Pieper 1967, 47–67; Samuelson 1972, n. 6). This
contrast, moreover, offers a way of handling the prickly problem
of future contingent events—one touchstone for Maimonides's
stark agnosticism. For if God knows everything, including future happenings, then their "not-yetness" has effectively been
undermined. If nothing is more sure than God's knowing, how
can it fail to determine what will happen? Here Aquinas makes
some decisive grammatical and linguistic prescriptions, which
I will offer in his terms and then present in my own. First a
preliminary observation: take care to translate every phrase

containing "future" as an adjective into a tensed verb phrase—so "my future job" becomes "the job I will take," *never* letting the adjective transform itself into a freestanding noun: "the future." (Whoever has lived even a short time among Arabs will recognize that the verbal expression calls immediately for *in sh'allah*—"God willing!"—and that's precisely the point of making the translation.) For a "future job" is a quite different animal from a "well-paying job" or a "boring job." Aquinas underscores the difference by noting that not even God can know "the future in itself"—that is, "what will be the case." For, as he puts it, "what-will-be—as what-will-be—does not yet have being (*esse*) in itself, and *truth* is convertible with *esse*. So, since all knowledge is of something true, it is impossible that any knowing which considers what-will-be in its respect of not-yet-being, can know it in itself" (*de Malo* [*Disputed Questions on Evil*] 16.7). (I have turned his statement about to make the point more dramatically—see Aquinas: *Q.D. de Veritate* [*Disputed questions on Truth*] 2.12.)

Yet he has also affirmed that God does know what-will-happen, so how can he slither out of this one? By insisting, of course, that God knows such things not as what-will-happen, but as happening. For "everything taking place in time is present to God in eternity, and not only to the extent that the essences (*rationes*) of things are present to God, but because his insight comprises all things from eternity, according as each thing is in its presentness" (*ST* 1.14.13). Here we have Aquinas's decisive step beyond a theory of emanation to God's knowledge of particulars, accomplished by a direct reference to a mode of being (and of knowing) quite opaque to us: eternity. It is the transformation (in the sense of relativity theory: the Lorentz transformations) effected by this shift of perspectives that will allow him to affirm coherently the five features of divine knowing that Maimonides listed as *givens*, and which Gersonides tried to dissolve. (The five features are: "first, that his knowledge is one, and yet embraces many different kinds of objects. Secondly, it is applied to things not in existence. Thirdly, it comprehends the infinite. Fourthly, it remains unchanged, though it comprises knowledge of changeable things. Fifthly, according to the teaching of our Law, God's knowledge of one of two eventualities does not determine it, however certain that knowledge may be of the occurrence of the one eventuality" [3.20].)

The resulting linguistic recommendation is telling: "If we want to convey the sense of God's way of knowing, it would he better to say that God knows this to be rather than [to say] that God knows what-will-be (*quod Deus scit hoc esse quam quod sciat futurum esse*), because things are never future to him but always present; . . . as it is more proper to speak of *providentia* than of *praevidentia*" (*de Ver* 2.12). "Our difficulty with all this, however, stems from the fact that we are unable to signify divine knowledge except through that mode proper to our own which [inevitably] consignifies differences in time" (*der Ver* 2.12).

Lest the direction these eminent figures take, transforming Job's pleas into the problematic of divine knowing, with all it attendant conundra—speculative/practical, temporal/eternal—seems a far cry from our concerns or Job's, we shall see it at work in the way in which Marilyn McCord Adams will find it necessary to expose the uniqueness of the creator/creature relation to clear the way for a strategic way of addressing "horrendous evils." So we shall learn how much we stand in need

of metaphysical reflection to help invert out normal expecta-
tions attending a relationship with God. For if that relation is
predicated on one of creative presence, that is, practical rather
than speculative reason, then there is a possibility of encounter
even with the source of all being. In short, normal expecta-
tions regarding "transcendence," which are inextricably tied to
distance and remoteness, are in fact utterly reversed. When the
eternal One is present to each temporally existing thing as the
source of its being, the present moment is the key to actuality.
After all, it is a profound redundancy to note that what exists,
exists *now*. This fact alone reminds us that despite that profound
"distinction" of Creator from all that is (created), the possibility of dialogue is inscribed in the creating relationship. For the
One who bestows existence as a free gift ought be susceptible
to being addressed as well as be capable of responding. The
"distinction," in other words, does not translate into an unbridge-
able gap. And that realization seems to have empowered Job's
daring pleas and bold requests, directed to the One who gives
him existence, even in the midst of affliction.

# 7

# JOB MEDIATING
# TWO OPPOSING VIEWS
# OF THEODICY

THE EXPLICIT AIM of this reflection has been to show how the book of Job effectively deconstructs sober efforts of philosophers to construct theories "justifying the ways of God to men" (quite oblivious of the irony in that description of their task). So it seems appropriate to use what we have gleaned from Job to assess the way two quite disparate recent explorations have each effectively employed astute philosophical strategies to deconstruct what had become known as "theodicy." In this way, we can fulfill the ancillary goal of this reflection: to show how scripture can hone our philosophical skills to yet more pointed results. Terrence Tilley's *Evils of Theodicy* (1991) and Marilyn McCord Adams's *Horrendous Evils* (1999) display quite different philosophical cultures, and might easily be seen as opposing each other: while Tilley trashes the very idea of *theodicy*, McCord Adams exposes how a set of strategies prevailing among current analytic philosophers of religion fail to meet their goals, and so endeavors to offer an alternative of her own. Yet describing her work that way fails to specify the purported goals of the endeavors she criticizes, goals nicely articulated by Tilley as "explaining how there could be evil in God's world" (2). For in fact McCord Adams expressly eschews that goal; *explaining* is not a strategy she adopts (or can adopt), once having shown how questionable are those that have recently been offered. Her central thesis rather focuses on the goodness of God, which alone can defeat "horrendous evils," yet her "strategy for showing how this can be done is to identify ways that created participation in horrors can be integrated into the participants' relation to God" (155). So what will be required is that we acknowledge the sui generis relation of creatures to a Creator, "understood to be the incommensurate Good," so as to personally enact and appropriate that relation in such a way that it be "overall incommensurately good *for the participant*" (155).

As formidable as the initial acknowledgment may be, what follows is even more critical: only performance will allow divine action to defeat the evil in question, and performance involves speech acts totally different from explanation. Tilley outlines the relevant speech-act strategies, employing them astutely to offer a reading of Job that removes that text from any possible pretence to explain God's hand in Job's affliction, yet the two apparently contrasting studies converge to endorse what the book of Job displays, by opposing Job's address *to* God to the discourse of his "friends" *about* God. Again, once apprised of the rich metaphysical context of the creator/creature relation, attempts to offer explanations will sound silly, so nothing short of enacting that ineffable relation will allow the creature so afflicted to "go on." A rich store of silliness can be found in the bevy of recent "explanations," many of which she shows to be wanting, for they purport (often for strategic reasons) to delineate the relation between "free agents" and a generic "God," quite oblivious to the founding relation of creation, thus sidestepping the rich metaphysical context that unique relation first demands and can then exploit. Although she does not spell it out, the "ability to go on," which one might identify as her proposal to meet the goals of "theodicy," must embody a quality of understanding of a radically different sort than explanations can provide. For even if Eliphaz and his companions are castigated for "not having spoken of [God] what is right as [his] servant Job has" (42:7), God cannot be commending Job for "getting it right," as we might say. For his cumulative outbursts are a far cry from attempts to explain his plight, never pretending to be more than bewildered complaints—despite the ways his "friends'" often construed them. What the voice from the whirlwind commends is rather the inherent rightness of Job's mode of discourse: speaking (however he may speak) *to* rather than *about* his creator. Furthermore, the entire divine peroration had just delineated majestically how creating is central to the scenario, and Job's multifarious complaints presume that it is the Creator he is daring to address. Indeed, that presumption alone was enough to raise the ire of his interlocutors.

Now both McCord Adams, by positive recommendation, and Tilley, by indirection, employ sophisticated theological strategies to lead us to this very point: that as creatures we

might dare to enter into this founding relation with the Creator who gives each of us our very being, and should we do so,
the personal boundlessness of that relation will allow us "to go
on." Tilley can be said to make this point only implicitly, in his
sensitive reading of the book of Job and of Augustine, each of
whom he shows decidedly not to be engaged in the distinctively
"modern undertaking [of] theodicy" (2). In contrasting the
contours of the poem, as well as Augustine's topical reflections
on the human situation, to modern renditions of "the problem
of evil," Tilley alludes to the rich context we have identified as
the creator/creature relation. McCord Adams is rather intent
on showing how purported "solutions" to "the problem" can
neatly bypass the fact of "horrendous evils," thereby displaying how inane is their way of proceeding in the face of realities we can name. And once having rendered such discussions
irrelevant, she proceeds to articulate, in richly metaphysical
language, the unique relation between the protagonists, creator
and creatures, notably intentional creatures. She must do so
because her brand of interlocutors invariably omits any such
considerations, presuming "God" and "human being" to be two
items to be related, each quite intelligible in its own right,
rather than two that are already internally related as creator
and creature. Indeed, one might speculate whether that fun-
damental oversight might have helped to spawn the enterprise
of "theodicy," marking it as "modern," since medieval thinkers
had been forced to work assiduously and collaboratively (as
Jews, Christians, and Muslims) to incorporate a free Creator
into the Hellenistic legacy they inherited (Burrell 1987). Yet
once we follow the invitation of the scriptures, Bible or Qur'an,
to identify God as Creator, whatever we say *about* God will

have to respect the distinctiveness of the creator/creature relation. Robert Sokolowski adopts phenomenological strategies
to delineate that distinctiveness as "the Christian distinction,"
though I have argued that we can find it in Judaism and Islam
as well (Sokolowski 1995; Burrell 1996).

In particular, this means that whenever God acts, God acts
as creator or conserver, and Aquinas reminds us that these two
names identify one mode of acting, differing from each other
only notionally: the action of conserving presupposes creation,
while creating presupposes nothing at all. Invoking this rule at
once renders all talk of the Creator "intervening" inappropriate,
as well as neutralizes debates over "compatibilism" or "determinism," since using the first term presumes two agents operating
within the same field of force, while the second presumes that
the causality in question is intramundane. Yet it must be em-
phasized that we are directed to this rich metaphysical mode
of reflection by the scriptures themselves, thereby reminding
all who would explore this domain that they cannot be less
than philosophical theologians. McCord Adams concludes her
extended essay by reminding us that her "strategy for dealing
with horrendous evils carries the corollary consequence of blur-
ring the boundary between philosophy and theology" (206).
Some fifty years ago Josef Pieper did the same for Thomists, by
identifying the "hidden element in the philosophy of Aquinas
as creation," yet neo-Thomist institutional boundaries were
so firmly established and enforced that it has taken that same
period for studies in Aquinas to celebrate his instinctive and pervasive indifference to the boundaries modernity later imposed.
Indeed, one can find startling affinities between postmodern
and medieval sensibilities (Burrell 2004a). So we should not be

surprised to find scripture demanding philosophical clarifica-
tions to display its own coherence, or philosophers turning to
scripture to illuminate their way of proceeding in these arcane
arenas. Moreover, once they make that "scriptural turn," they
will also be led to deconstruct some other ways of proceeding
to which philosophers had become accustomed. That represents the patent subtext of McCord Adams's reflections, as
well as the avowed goal of our reflection. (I have been able
to rely throughout on astute readings of Job, in a similar vein,
communicated to me by Eleanor Stump.)

In that vein, let us resume Tilley's penetrating reading of Job,
as it carefully distinguishes among the plethora of speech-acts
in Job's rich repertory, to reach his assessment of the way this
book can illuminate the enterprise of theodicy. As in McCord
Adams, sophisticated philosophical analysis is put to the service of unveiling the senses of scripture, which of course invites
contentious interaction as well as appreciation. After following
the dramatic sequences of linguistic events, much as we have in
chapter 2, Tilley employs his speech-act categories (italicized
in this excerpt) to essay the following summary of the progress
to Job's final peroration just before Elihu's intervention (chs.
29–31):

> Job has moved from curse, lament, and complaint to consider-
> ing legal "action, even if that action is an impossible dream"
> (Habel 1985). [Indeed,] Job has moved from the "weakest"
> type of speech act, his expressive lament, to the strongest,
> his terrible declaration of his final oath and the audacious
> directive of his challenge to God. How his actions shifted
> from lament to oath can be illumined by considering the
> speech acts he performed along the way. Job's *assertions*

focus on three content areas. First, they center on his miserable situation. Job constantly asserts that God is the cause of his misery (e.g., 9–10), using violent metaphors of wounding (6:4, 16:12–14), assault (19:7), dethroning ((19:9), and battle (19:12) to accuse God, although Job maintains his innocence (e.g., 9:21, 27:7). Second, Job frequently recalls the miserable human plight of the God-given human condition he shares (7:1–10, 12:5–25, 14:1–6, 21, 24). Third, Job generally agrees with much of his comforters' theology, but compares their torments with those God inflicts on him (19:22) and directly contradicts Eliphaz's key assertion of retributive justice (24). Save for this third group, there is little development in Job's *assertions*.

Nor is there much development in Job's *directives*. He frequently challenges God or his friends to inform him, he sometimes begs pity of both, and his final oath concludes with a defiant challenge to God.

Yet Job's *expressives* change remarkably. He begins with curse (3:1) and lament (3, 6:2–3), but no further curse is expressed and subsequent laments over his suffering are brief (e.g., 10:1) or conclude descriptions of the human condition (7:11–16). His expressive lament seems supplanted by *assertive accusations*. He later begins his speech expressively insulting and deriding his comforters (12:2–5, 13:1–5, 16:1–5, 26:2–4). He expresses some hope for a witness (16:18–17:1) but soon utters a cry of despair (17:11–16). But when he returns to lament (23), he no longer centers on his suffering, but now laments God's immunity from arraignment. It is as if the legal metaphors which structure Job's speeches in his dialogues with the comforters (e.g., 14:13–17) shift the focus of the feelings to which Job gives vent (94).

Without delving too deeply into its internal structure, readers should be able to appreciate the usefulness of this semantic strategy, which turns on classifying and identifying speech acts. For our purposes, Tilley's deft use of the strategy can help readers of the Job text to attend to various modes of expression, thereby discriminating various stages in his extended lament. Tilley continues:

> Job makes three *declarations* in his speeches. They are linked with the only *commissive* which he issues. They are also linked with *directives*. His first is the "arraignment" of God in 13:19 to contend against him. He asks God to withdraw his pressure and dread and demands that God tell him his offense and sin (13:23). . . . His second *declaration* is both an *illocutionary denegation* (an explicit *declaration* that one is *not* performing a speech act . . .) and a positive *declaration*: he refuses to find his comforters right and maintains his innocence (27:5–6). . . . His third *declaration* is his *oath/confession* of his innocence . . . with *imprecations* (31:7–12, 38–40). He challenges/summons God, his adversary at law, to appear, and commits himself to flaunt whatever God writes—an inscription which the text leaves ambiguous, for God may write an indictment of Job or a verdict of acquittal (94–95).

At this point Tilley signals the fact that "God startlingly speaks to Job from the whirlwind," adding that "God shockingly also responds to Job's act of summoning God" (95). Then he proceeds to concern himself with the proper interpretation of Job's response to God's second speech: "I had heard of you by the hearing of the ear, but now my eye has seen you. Therefore I retreat and I repent in dust and ashes" (42:5–6). Offering eight differing translations, Tilley can only conclude that Job is silenced; and what is more, he contends summarily that

> if one takes Job's position when one comes to read the text of Job, or if one takes Job's perspective as the key to reading Job, and if one enacts Job, then one is silenced. Moreover, it is God as portrayed in Job who does the silencing (102).

Furthermore, since God directs his commendation of Job to Eliphaz, Tilley presumes that "God never lets Job know he spoke rightly" (98), so God's own address (42:7), which "endorses Job's speaking . . . is worthless" (102).

On the basis of this presumption—"all we can know is that God never lets Job know he spoke rightly"—with Job's inconclusive riposte to God's cosmic revelation (which amounts to acknowledging that he has been silenced by the very One who did respond to him), Tilley concludes that the book of "Job warns against the possibility of providing a theodicy" (109). Yet we should want to explore more directly Tilley's being shocked and startled that God responded to Job. Is this very fact not worth more than vain attempts to glean the exact meaning of the words from the whirlwind, which (rightly, I believe) Tilley does not spend much time parsing. For "all we can know" (to parse Tilley) is that no set of words, however poetic, could ever claim to offer the sense of God's direct response to Job, or to Job's request that God respond, even though the protocols of a written text demand that both be somehow recorded. Yet does not the drama inherent in Job's direct invocation to God, together with God's responding directly to him and then commending that very mode of invocation, demand that we focus on these performatives before anything else? And if we do so, neither God's address itself nor his endorsement of Job's direct address could ever be counted "worthless." Unless, of course, one be mesmerized by the very enterprise of *theodicy*, narrowly construed as "explaining how there could be evil in God's world." On that account, Tilley scores neatly against a plethora of attempts in current "philosophy of religion," yet this present attempt to show how the book of Job might alter our very conception of *theodicy*, together with the suggested reading of McCord Adams's fresh initiative, should lead us well beyond *explanation* as a paradigm for making sense of even "horrendous evils," however we may then want to employ the term *theodicy*.

Moreover, anyone who wishes to continue to use the term may be helped by Rowan Williams's interview with Rupert Shortt, which offers a way of clarifying his objections to an earlier presentation of this subject by McCord Adams (to which she alludes in her book):

> SHORTT: One of Marilyn Adams' arguments in the exchange you've had with her is that, *sub specie aeternitatis*, we will find that our lives are retrospectively vindicated, justified. Isn't that implicit in Christian belief? . . . .
>
> WIILLIAMS: "Vindicated": that's where I have the problem. I may look back on an experience of enormous trauma and say, Well, out of that came some understanding for which I thank God. What I can't bring myself to say is that, so to speak, it was all OK. I can't quite cope with the idea that somebody else's suffering was planned for a good purpose.
>
> SHORTT: But you believe that creation is ultimately a good thing.

WILLIAMS: I believe that creation is a good thing because of that long-term purpose which is the sharing of fellowship with God, the gift of divine life and the divine nature to creatures. But to say that creation is good overall, I think, can't commit us to adding, All that happens must be for the best. Not only is that often not true; even when we can make the best of a bad situation, that doesn't mean that it had to happen or that it was good that it happened. I look here to those who have written out of very dark places of the modern experience. One thinks of somebody like Etty Hillesum writing from the camps, or on the Christian side Mother Maria Skobtsova, a Russian nun who died in Ravensbruck, and what I understand them to be saying is not, Well, it's all OK, there's a reason for my being here, but rather, Here is something which for all its utter, unqualified horror, I can by God's grace give a future to, open up to God. And in that sense, I think, the Christian looking back over a life containing suffering and tragedy and trauma can say that it has all been drawn together by grace, rather than that it's all vindicated or justified (Shortt 2005, 12–13).

Again, whatever understanding may be forthcoming is thoroughly operative, as in Wittgenstein's "knowing how to go on," a quality of understanding that one might relate retrospectively to oneself, without ever proposing that it could assist another prospectively.

Understanding of this sort diverges utterly from that of *explanation* (even if philosophers tend to equate understanding with explaining). Indeed, sharing such understanding with another could be quite salutary to that person, but the effect of relating it can never be predicted. Now it appears that McCord Adams's latest attempt respects that fact, as her "strategy for showing

how this can be done is to identify ways that created participation in horrors can be integrated into the participants' relation
to God" (155). Yet the sense of "can be" must be focused by the
italics she supplies to the words that will end this sentence, so
that one who acknowledges the sui generis relation of creatures
to a Creator, "understood to be the incommensurate Good,"
will have to enact and appropriate that relation in such a way
that it be "overall incommensurately good *for the participant*"
(155). Certainly no account, however sophisticated, can effect
that appropriation when even personal exchange cannot as-
sure it. Yet it does seem that a proper grasp of the "distinction"
between creator and creatures will be required to effect it, for
failing to acknowledge the sui generis relation of creatures to
a creator can lead to endless queries of why "God is doing this
to me," where the "God" in question is simply presumed to be
another actor on the scene. Moreover, McCord Adams's latest
effort displays this signal difference in the way she explicitly
articulates, in richly metaphysical language, the unique relation
between the Creator and creatures, and notably intentional
creatures. While her chapter 4, entitled "Divine Agency Re-
modeled," may appear to be a digression, I read it as an implicit
critique of the insouciance of "philosophers of religion" to this
signal fact, and now wish to link her concerns with the book of
Job as well. For despite his railing, Job never doubts that he is
contending with the creator-God, one whom his interlocutors
insisted on announcing as beyond human reach even while
they never doubted their capacity to articulate the pattern of
his actions.

Now common objections to this contention abound, of
course: how can Job (or we) talk *to* so metaphysical a God?

Moreover, is not the entire book cast in the covenantal mode, so portraying God as interacting with creatures? And does not God answer Job, thereby showing that he is a person? So the list will continue until it invariably underscores the touted opposition between "Greek" and "Hebrew" modes of thought. Many recent commentators have conspired to nullify that abstraction, however, the most constructive attempt being Robert Sokolowski's genial introduction of "the Christian distinction" in his *God of Faith and Reason*. For he shows how the sui generis "distinction" of Creator from creatures was celebrated in liturgical life long before it was articulated doctrinally; and in fact its conciliar articulations were always distillations of practice. Indeed, "Greek metaphysics" played so critical a role in unfolding the Christian tradition that it can hardly be read as an intrusion. Moreover, its initial role was to preserve the *schema*: "Hear, O Israel, God your God is One!" (Deut. 6:4), in the face of Christian practice acknowledging in myriad ways the divinity of Jesus (Weinandy, 1985). The Council of Nicaea (325) affirmed the Word of God (made human in Jesus) to be "of one substance with the Father," while Chalcedon (451) specified the ontological constitution of Jesus as "two natures in one 'person.'" Beginning with the uniqueness of Jesus, Hellenic theological language would then be utilized to sharpen the sense in which the creator-God could never be said to be part of creation, thereby confirming Jewish strictures against idolatry, and (later) Muslim strictures against "associating anything [created] with the one God" [*shirk*]. These shared concerns of Jews, Christians, and Muslims culminated in medieval efforts to secure the Creator as the One who freely emanates the universe, with special attention to the assertions of the Bible and

Qur'an that insisted on an initial moment of time (Burrell 1986, 1993). So the revelational language of both Bible and Qur'an would require, for its elaboration in practice, some clarification employing a philosophical idiom, though each of these faith traditions would count on key thinkers from their midst to render that philosophy complementary to revelation.

Yet philosophers have regularly chafed at playing a role complementary to revelation, preferring to legislate the limits of scriptural language according to their operative categories. And inversely, some "Christian philosophers" have insisted that the very language of scripture demands that God be treated as an interlocutor concurring in human endeavors, so displaying their innocence of the conciliar developments just noted, which carefully adapted philosophy to disambiguate the narrative language of scripture. For terms like *interlocutor* and *concurrence* presume agents operating on the same level, whereas the covenant of the creator-God with the people Israel is suffused with the free initiative of the One establishing it. Indeed, this has been our initial presumption: the book of Job serves as a corrective to casual idolatrous constructions of Deuteronomy, by which covenantal transactions are taken to be quite automatic, so effacing the ever-present personal initiative of the Creator. So a pattern of inquiry whereby "philosophers of religion" egregiously overlook this founding "distinction" (of creator/creatures) will perforce lead them into idolatry by unwittingly "associating" the divinity with creatures; a double irony when that strategy purports to find scriptural warrant by accepting narrative modes of scriptural discourse at face value. Yet as we have seen, each Abrahamic tradition found it necessary to have recourse to sophisticated hermeneutics to render its practice articulate, and thereby secure what is distinctive in its revelation. Similarly, McCord Adams will find it necessary to "estimat[e] what sort of agency it would take to defeat horrors within the context of the individual participant's life" (60).

In this she clearly acknowledges how latent presumptions about the "kind of actor" God is, including those regarding "divine moral goodness" (59) have set the stage for much standard theodicy. She had initially presented the high metaphysical accounts of the Creator as "cause of being" as those of her interlocutors and so avoided endorsing them. Yet she will later find it necessary to incorporate that very perspective in presenting what she sees as her more "personal" account of divine agency, precisely "to confront and undermine the charge that personhood in this sense is necessarily leveling, that it would automatically shrink God down to anthropomorphic giant-size" (81).[1] Moreover, all this sounds just right, for a keen sense of the uniqueness of the One about whom one is attempting to speak, or to whom one is daring to address oneself, will doubtless help to eliminate much nonsense of the "why is God doing this to me?" variety. For while the "why" makes eminent sense as a plea or even a complaint, it does not as a request for an

---

1. McCord Adams relies upon Paul Tillich, David Burrell, and Katherine Tanner to "remodel divine agency," displaying a prior familiarity with Tillich as well as a sensitive reading of the latter two, even if their work is summarized with reference to a single article of each. The most egregious misreading is of Tanner, who is led to say that "God exercises full control by direct action to produce creatures acting in a certain way," and is said to insist "that created freedom is compatible with Divine determinism, since the distinction between natural and free, free and coerced, is a matter of how created causes relate to one another" (68). McCord Adams's use of "control" and especially of "Divine determinism" in a context where Tanner's clear distinction should have forced her to eschew such "leveling" terms, offers unwitting testimony of the way categories developed independent of a creator will inevitably be inappropriately used in the face of a creator, leading one to make statements counter to the unique reality of the creator/creature relation.

explanation. For the action of a creator-God simply will not fit into anticipated explanatory frames, any more than the activity of creating can be parsed as a process. Indeed, as we saw in chapter 6, comparisons with classical commentaries in Christian and other religious traditions may well be able to elicit those further resources, in each tradition, which Marilyn McCord Adams finds in Christianity.

# 8

# ASSESSING JOB'S CONTRIBUTION TO THEODICY

## Contrasting Semantics of Explaining and Addressing

ETURNING TO THE book of Job in the context of the Hebrew Bible, it seems quite clear now that the poet has little to offer for one who defines *theodicy* (as Terrence Tilley quite standardly does) as "explaining how there could be evil in God's world." For the only ones who attempt to *explain* Job's plight are his friends-turned-tormenters. Yet far from concluding that the poem is useless for addressing the issues of undeserved suffering at the hands of a creator-God (as Tilley ironically seems to do), we find that it rather directs us to eschew *explanation* for yet other ways of rendering enigmas intelligible. Here, Tilley's astute reminder of

forms of discourse other than the propositional suggests how
the poem can lead us to enlightenment in such recondite matters. Job is commended in the end because he dared to address
the creator-God; his interlocutors are castigated for purporting
to speak knowingly about that One. Speaking *about* something
veers toward explaining, while speaking *to* someone can engage
both in a relationship of exchange open to yet other forms
of understanding. Indeed, what is most telling, structurally,
in the book of Job is that the creator-God does answer Job's
extended complaints. Yet those looking for an explanation will
find themselves scrutinizing *what* the voice from the whirlwind
says, while the dynamic of the unfolding relationship should
lead us to what is most startling of all: *that* God responded to
him. As Wittgenstein remarked at the end of the *Tractatus*: "not
*how* the world is is the mystical, but *that* it is" (1961 6.44). In
like manner, Aquinas's insistence that "the proper effect of the
creator is the very existing of things" suggests a proper appreciation of the ineffable creator-creature relation (*ST* 1.45.4). So
obvious a reading of the book of Job not only offers a way to
deconstruct the elaborate explanations that have been proffered
as theodicy, but does so by accentuating (in poetic form) the
animadversions directed by both Aquinas and Wittgenstein to
thinkers so intent on "the way the world is" that the mystery
of its very existence can easily escape them.

Indeed, both performatively and thematically, God's act of
responding to Job mirrors the Creator's utterly spontaneous
"speaking" the universe "in the beginning"—the signal point of
Saadiah's commentary. And when one can address the creator-
God and be answered, standard theodicy has a chance of being
transformed in the way so carefully outlined by Marilyn McCord

Adams: "identify[ing] ways that created participation in horrors can be integrated into the participants' relation to God." Here, *theodicy*—if we can continue to call it that—does not pretend to offer an explanation. Yet it can direct us to ways of activating that "non-reciprocal relation of dependence" that defines our very creaturehood, thereby transforming the *fact* of our existing into an undeserved gift. Metaphysically, this move makes of our very existence an "existence-to" the Creator, as Aquinas cannily puts it, thereby transforming Aristotle's central definition of *substance* as "what exists in itself," in the face of a creator-God.[1] So McCord Adams was rightly advised to outline alternative attempts to articulate this ineffable relation of creator/creature, before attempting to offer some illumination into "horrendous evils." Indeed, as Saadiah noted, activating that relation as best we can will itself illumine a way of understanding utterly different from explaining. And that is precisely what Job does, so that the creator-God's responding to Job's sustained plea expresses the distinctively Jewish modality of covenant as well as mirrors the initial and enduring "speaking-creating," so as to fold the sheer gift of creation into an ongoing relationship of ritual response. Nor can this be accidental to the composition and construction of the book of Job, for (as we have seen) its primary function in the Hebrew canon may well be to correct "mechanical" readings of the Deuteronomy that remain heedless of the graceful divine initiative the covenant embodies. Here, of course, the target is not theologians so much as religious leaders, epitomized in Job's companions, who invariably attempt to

---

1. Aristotle, *Metaphysics* 7.6 (1032a5): "clearly, each primary and self-subsistent thing is one and the same as its essence." Aquinas, *ST* 1.45.3: "creation in things is a relation to their origin such that their very existence is an 'existence-to-the-creator.'"

channel God's generous initiative into manageable patterns. Yet taken as two phases of a single divine act, creation and covenant epitomize that "act of pure grace by which the Absolute God gave being where there need to have been none," as Goodman paraphrases Saadiah (99).

As if to compound the ironic effect of the poem, it is the non-Jewish Job who calls our attention to this unalloyed divine initiative on behalf, first, of the people Israel, and potentially of all human creatures. Similarly, the canonical Hebrew Bible begins with creation, postponing the archaic beginnings of Israel's story with Abraham to chapter 12, so reminding us that the God in question was not simply the Jewish god, the property of one tribe one among others, but also that all human beings are creatures who owe their utmost allegiance to the very source of their being. Yet since the covenant of this creator-God with Israel represents an unmistakable privileging of this people, Saadiah reminds us that the travails of Job will also be evidenced in the people Israel, while the poem itself shows that neither these travails nor the pattern of response to them that the non-Jewish Job embodies can be the property of any single person or people. Indeed, the manner in which Job's complaints, taken together with the creator-God's free response, set up a dialogic pattern for transforming our impulse to theodicy can be illuminated by the extended second-person narrative of Augustine's *Confessions* (or as Gary Wills renders the title, his *Testimony*). There is no dearth of explanatory passages in Augustine's narrative of discovery, yet they are invariably offered as a way of facilitating the next step he sees that he must take, while the entire context is one of prayer to God, punctuated by realizations about God. As in the book of Job, the pervasive second-person dialogic context sets the stage for action, while those who overhear it can glean both personal and speculative fruit from the exchange.

## A Comparison with Augustine's *Confessions*

Augustine opens his *Confessions* asserting:

> Man is one of your creatures, Lord, and his instinct is to praise you. . . . The thought of you stirs him so deeply that he cannot be content unless he praises you, because you made us for yourself and our hearts find no peace until they rest in you. (Augustine, 1961 1.1)

These words begin a reflective introduction of five short chapters to a work that some have regarded as a paradigm for autobiography. Yet it differs from modern autobiographies in its form of address and its attribution of agency. It frequently shifts from first to second person, as its author is moved to praise, since Augustine's narrative activity of remembering is less preoccupied with what happened to him and how he negotiated it than with (1) identifying the sources of power and once located, (2) learning how to receive from that source. If *autobiography*, like *autonomy*, suggests to us a self centered on itself, Augustine's journey delivers a self related to its source and only then ordered in itself—since to be related to one's source and goal *is* to be properly ordered with oneself. Seeking and receiving are reciprocally related, since recognizing *what* and *who* that source is orients one to the proper ways to receive from it. So if the self Augustine articulates is not autonomous but related, the form of his articulation will be dialogic. Yet how are the two—form and substance—related? My interpretative hypothesis asks us to attend to three factors, each features of the work. The first is a simple reminder that introductions are written once we have finished composing, for only then can we confidently say where we wish to go. So the assertion that introduces the narrative—a second-person assertion, at that—is best thought of as the fruit of sustained efforts to articulate his journey of relating. And those efforts—my second premise—constitute an experiment: an account of a life becomes an "experiment in truth," while the narrative mode of accounting enhances the experiment by articulating it for us. Finally, the response of God to Augustine's sustained yet fitful outreach is exhibited in the life itself—that is, in what God accomplished in him by way of right ordering. Book 10 offers a current "progress report" on that transformation, replete with Augustine's disappointment at its incompleteness, yet the fact of what has been accomplished encourages him to move beyond his own narrative to the cosmic commentary of books 11–13, thereby articulating the ground for his opening assertion: "Man is one of your creatures, Lord, and his instinct is to praise you."

So the propriety of the dialogic form of the narrative-recollection that is the *Confessions* is corroborated as the reality of each partner comes more into evidence through exercises in dialogue: here it is Augustine speaking and God working. What is more, each protagonist is seen to be dialogic in nature: with God, the dialogue is reflected more in God's interaction with creation than within divinity itself (as in his *de Trinitate*); with Augustine, it is exhibited primarily in communal exchange with friends, with Monica, and with his son.[2] This feature of his narrative, notably evident after he leaves Africa for Italy, reminds us forcibly that this "autobiography" does not render an "autonomous individual" but a person-in-community.[3] The character of that community proves to be the crucial middle term in the verification that Augustine seeks in trying to identify accurately the source of right order, capable of restoring himself and the world to its original ordering. For he comes to see how participating in such a community offers the most promising hope for attaining an ordered self, as its teachings offer a paradigm for assessing alternative accounts of world order. (Hence, the apt observation of readers who have seen in this work the itinerary of a journey toward "joining the church.") To ask what kind of a community it is that he embraces (and by which he *is* embraced), however, is not to be directed to historical "proofs" but to be directed to ask: what sort of life does that community exhibit? The response, especially of book 8, is that it generates saints: exemplary individuals who exhibit an enviable ordering in their lives. (Indeed, one is reminded of the thesis developed by Patrick Sherry, "that the *absence* of such holy people over time could put a community's claims to question" [Sherry 1984].) The community can be said to generate them, since we find this ordering in people who identify themselves as followers of Jesus. It is an ordering,

2. The relation with his long-term mistress is notoriously more problematic. His most inadvertent, and so most authentic, confession may be the indirect discourse he employs to relate how "the woman with whom I had been living was torn from my side as an obstacle to my marriage." Although he goes on to acknowledge that "this was a blow which crushed my heart to bleeding, because I loved her dearly" (6.15), does the initial "was torn" represent our usual ruse to avoid responsibility in the matter?

3. I am indebted to an unpublished study by my colleague Frederick J. Crosson: "Cicero and Augustine," delivered at a colloquium at Notre Dame, 1985.

moreover, which exemplifies the best of human nature, yet is all too seldom exemplified in individual human beings. So those bonded in this community—the "body of Christ"—testify to the presence and activity of the original orderer of the world, as well as to the further fact that individuals can relate to such a One: "You made us for yourself and our hearts find no peace until they rest in you" (1.1).

So much for the structure of the *Confessions;* how does it work? That, of course, is what the narrative is designed to show in his case. But what about us? What if our story—yours or mine—does not so conclude? Is that not the way with stories, in principle? They are not "universalizable." Or are there certain ones that are paradigmatic for the rest of us? Archetypal, even, so that we cannot escape incorporation into their plot? These would be "everyman" stories, enlightening us regarding our origins and our destiny. And even if we would admit such stories, would Augustine's *Confessions* be among them? Can his story be archetypal, however much some of us would like it to be? Here it is useful to contrast the direction Augustine's journey took with a path it could have taken, at the penultimate milestone of the journey toward discovery. His is not an account, as the story of his Platonist guides would be, of the necessary ascent of a human soul to its inherent perfection, impeded only by willful inattention or blindness. It rather spells out a free response to an invitation freely offered to each person and avowedly to all, yet the story unfolds into a willing response enfolded within a dynamic initiated by the Other. The narrative-recollection as Augustine offers it, then, may be paradigmatic but is not archetypal. That is, it can help to structure your story, but it cannot be said to structure it inescapably. So not only is it experimental in Augustine's case; it is inherently experimental: try it on, to see whether your story can be modeled upon it. The *promise* is that yours will be able so to be modeled, if you but try. The incentive lies in your observation that those who have, and are otherwise like you, exhibit an enviable ordering, so why not try? At least those who participate in the same community with Augustine can hope to find that incentive.

If that is all we can glean from this exercise with Augustine, however, to what end? There seems to be little, if anything, new here. What has our study of the form and function of Augustine's *Confessions* succeeded in showing? Two things, I shall suggest, that may be more therapeutic than startling. The first regards the indispensability of narrative, especially first-person narrative, in framing an account of an invitation offered freely so that it elicits a willing response. Any other form of discourse, it seems, will tend to eclipse the free dynamic of invitation and response in favor of some mode of explanation. The second is a corollary of the first: the centrality of friendship and of dialogue in human life will elicit a rich second-person discourse, opening one up to the possibility, if not the fact of such an exchange with the one source of all. The shorthand expression for such a relationship with God is "grace," and the contrast that Augustine finds between his Platonist guides and those who witness faith in Jesus as the Word of God, epitomized in the tonal differences between Books 7 and 8 of the *Confessions,* displays the novelty that he discovers *grace* to be. The fruit of that new power in his personal life is a transformed vision of the world itself, where all things have "the same message to tell, if only we can hear it, and their message is this:

We did not make ourselves, but [the One] who abides forever made us" (9.10). Having negotiated the journey he recounts, Augustine is now able to hear this response from the things whose beauty he admires.

Comparing this development, as it is articulated by Augustine, with that of Job elicits palpable analogies, notably in enlisting first- and second-person discourse to articulate the way, both for themselves and as their stories unfold, for others. Yet the most striking disanalogy lies in the presence of friends with Augustine at key points in his life, along with his realizing their indispensability for his own journey, contrasted with the way Job's companions turn out to be the very opposite of friends. Yet they did not start that way. When they first arrived, "they sat with him on the round seven days and seven nights, and no one spoke a word to him, for they saw that his suffering was very great" (2:11). What happened, then? What made them so alter their character? There is, of course, a simple human answer: we all get tired of waiting in incomprehension, so must suitably explain things, first to ourselves, so that we can go on. Yet one might also essay a thematic answer: if these "friends" were to represent "teachers in Israel" (as their magisterial tone suggests), then the poet's depiction of the absence of a community to sustain Job in his suffering would correspond to the prophets' consistent excoriation of Israel's leaders for their failure to heed God's promises and activity in the life of the people. Yet if the community that Augustine was blessed to find was all too often absent in the history of Israel, it can be scarce in the unfolding of the "new Israel" as well. So it may not be that Job needs to be alone to stand out as heroic, but that he is forced to do so. Understood in this way, the poem takes to task religious leaders and theologians alike.

## Integrating Creation

Yet Job 's experience teaches what those creatures who seek to relate to their creator discover for themselves: that it is quite unlike beating a path to another's door, for there is literally no distance at all between creature and creator if the very being of every creature is a "being-to" its source. In this case, then, relating is not so much a task as it is a surrender to the "facts of the matter," a letting-go of a posture of "existential autonomy" (or separateness) to submit to the innate desire toward "the Good" that spells our fulfillment. Relating to the Creator, then, is like a free fall, yet for intentional beings, the term *free* has a double connotation: not only unhindered, but deliberate as well. That is the dynamic that Augustine's *Confessions* articulate, and the one that the creator-God's response to Job makes evident—to him and to us. We have already articulated the way Saadiah identifies free creation as the primary revelation of the book of Job. Yet it may also help to enlist the assistance of a theologian who immersed herself in the thought of Sankara, as well as the practice of prayer associated with this Hindu tradition, Sara Grant. In her *Towards an Alternative Theology*, she has argued for adapting Sankara's arresting term "nonduality" to render the "non-reciprocal relation of dependence," which Aquinas insists creation must be (Grant 2002, 40). So we are led to see how a proper grasp of the act of creating must be ingredient in a proper grasp of the act of self-revealing (for Muslims), as well as a proper grasp of the act of covenanting (for Jews), and a proper grasp of the act of incarnating (for Christians). Indeed, only a creator could unite with created nature without contradiction, since creator and creature cannot be two separate things. Indeed, it is illustrative to note how the Qur'an proposes, pairwise, the resurrection of the body as "evidence" of creation, and creation as "proof" of the resurrection, so that accepting one in faith stands or falls with accepting the other.

So the upshot of each of these revelations is to move their faithful into new ways of speaking and thinking about the universe of which we are a part, as well as our part in it. About the universe, "by the introduction of a new distinction, the distinction between the world understood as possibly not having existed—[recall Aristotle's presumption that the universe always was]—and God understood as possibly being all there is, with no diminution of goodness or greatness. It is not the case that God and the world are each separately understood in this new way, and only subsequently related to each other; they are determined in the distinction, not each apart from the other." So "God is understood not only to have created the world, but to have permitted the distinction between himself and the world to occur" (Sokolowski 1995, 23, 33). As microcosms of the universe, our very being will entail learning how, in whatever we do, to return everything to the One from whom we received everything—by Torah-observance for Jews, by following Jesus for Christians, and by "Islam" for Muslims. So our life becomes our own, as our actions become free, when we respond freely to the invitation divinely proffered. Aligned with a metaphysics of creation, authentic freedom consists in a servant's response to God's call, a response issuing from an act of faith in a free Creator, given distinctive voice in each Abrahamic tradition, yet here displayed in the book of Job.

So let us consider the theological reflection on these matters found in Sara Grant's Teape lectures:

> In India as in Greece, the ultimate question must always be that of the relation between the supreme unchanging Reality and the world of coming-to-be and passing away, the eternal Self and what appears as non-Self, and no epistemology can stand secure as long as this question remains unanswered. [It is indeed this startling contention which this essay has been exploring with Job.] . . . A systematic study of Sankara's use of relational terms made it quite clear to me that he agrees with St. Thomas Aquinas in regarding the relation between creation and the ultimate Source of all being as a *non-reciprocal dependence relation;* i.e., a relation in which subsistent effect or "relative absolute" is *dependent on its cause for its very existence as a subsistent entity,* whereas the cause is *in no way dependent on the effect for its subsistence,* though there is a *necessary logical relation between cause and effect;* i.e., a relation which is *perceived by the mind* when it reflects on the implications of the existence of the cosmos (2002, 40, emphasis added).

Her final observation about a "necessary logical relation" is quite compatible with regarding creating as a free action of the creator, for its import is intended to capture Aquinas's identification of "creation in the creature [as] nothing other than a relation of sorts to the creator as the principle of its existing" (*ST* 1.45.3).

So the very existence (*esse*) of a creature is an *esse-ad*, an existing which is itself a relation to its source. As we have noted, nothing could better express the way in which Aquinas's reformulation of Avicenna's essence/existing distinction transforms Aristotle than to point out that what for Aristotle "exists in itself"' (substance) is for Aquinas derived from an Other in its very in-itselfness, or substantiality. Yet since the Other is the cause of being, each thing that exists-to the creator also exists in itself, for derived existence is no less substantial when it is derived from the One-who-is; so it remains possible to inquire into existing things without explicitly referring them to their source. "The distinction," in other words, need not *appear*. But that simply reminds us how unique a nonreciprocal relation of dependence must be, for only one relation can be so character-ized: that of creatures to creator. If creator and creature were distinct from each other in an ordinary way, the relation—even one of dependence—could not be nonreciprocal; for ordinar-ily the fact that something depends on an originating agent, as a child from a parent, must mark a difference in that agent itself. Yet the fact that a cause of being, properly speaking, is not affected by causing all-that-is does not imply remoteness or uncaring; indeed, quite the opposite. For such a One must cause in such a way as to be present in each creature as the one to which it is oriented in its very existing. In that sense, this One cannot be considered as *other* than what it creates, in an ordinary sense of that term, just as the creature's "being-to-the creator" [*esse-ad*] assures that it cannot *be* separately from its source (Burrell 1993, 112). So it will not work simply to contrast creation to emanation, or to picture the Creator distinct (in the ordinary sense) from creation by contrast with a more panthe-istic image. Indeed, it is to avoid such infelicities of imagination that Sara Grant has recourse to Sankara's sophisticated notion of *non-duality* to call our attention in an arresting way to the utter uniqueness of "the distinction" that must hold between creator and creation, but cannot be pictured in a contrastive manner.

Indeed, there are signal affinities between Sara Grant's mode of expression and Kathryn Tanner's sense of transcendence, in that both are expressly "non-contrastive."

Nor does Aquinas feel any compunction at defining creation as the "emanation of all of being from its universal cause [*emanatio totius entis a cause universali*]" (*ST* 1.45.1). Indeed, once he had emptied the emanation scheme of any mediating role, he could find no better way of marking the uniqueness of the causal relation of creation than using the term *emanation* to articulate it (Burrell 1987, 86–91). For once the scheme has been gutted, that sui generis descriptor should serve to divert us from imaging the Creator over-against the universe, as an entity exercising causal efficacy on anything-that-is in a manner parallel to causation within the universe (Hasker 1989). While the all-important "distinction" preserves God's freedom in creating, which the emanation scheme invariably finesses, we must nevertheless be wary of picturing that distinction in a fashion that assimilates the Creator to another item within the universe. Harm Goris has shown how close attention to the uniqueness of the creator/creature relation, with its attendant corollary of participation as a way of articulating this sui generis causal relation, can neutralize many of the conundra that continue to bedevil philosophers of religion (Goris 1996).

Although it may seem that we have strayed far from Augustine and Aquinas—to say nothing of Job!—in invoking Shakara's hybrid term of *non-duality*, we should have realized by now how much we need to help ourselves to various ways of expressing the inexpressible: the *distinction* as well as the *relation* between creatures and their creator. Both prove to be foundational to any attempt to grasp our transcendent origins as gift. Bible and

Qur'an conspire to highlight the creator's freedom; philosophy proves helpful in finding ways to think both creature and creator together. Job offers a poignant poetic rendition of the inexpressible relation, personally executed in the heart of affliction.

Leo the Great (c. 400–61) offers a Christian recapitulation of the message of this book in a sermon for the feast celebrating the transfiguration of Jesus:

> The writings of the two testaments support each other. The radiance of the transfiguration reveals clearly and unmistakably the one who had been promised by signs foretelling him under the veils of mystery. As Saint John says: "the law was given through Moses, grace and truth came through Jesus Christ." In him the promise made through the shadows of prophecy stands revealed, along with the full meaning of the precepts of the law. He is the one who teaches the truth of prophecy through his presence, and makes obedience to the commandments possible through grace. In the preaching of the holy gospel all should receive a strengthening of their faith. No one should be ashamed of the cross of Christ, through which the world has been redeemed. No one should fear to suffer for the sake of justice; no one should lose confidence in the reward that has been promised. The way to rest is through toil, the way to life is through death. Christ has taken upon himself the whole weakness of our lowly human nature. If then we are steadfast in our faith in him and in our love for him, we win the victory that he has won, we receive what he has promised. When it comes to obeying the commandments or enduring adversity, the words uttered by the Father should always echo in our ears: "This is my Son, the beloved, in whom I am well pleased; listen to him." (Sermon 51, 3–4, 8, *Patrologia Latina* 54, 310–11, 313)

# BIBLIOGRAPHY

Adams, Marilyn McCord. 1999 *Horrendous Evils and the Goodness of God*. Ithaca, NY: Cornell University Press.

Aquinas, Thomas. 1965. *Expositio super Job ad litteram*. Rome: Ad Sanctam Sabinam.

Augustine, Saint. 1961. *Confessions*, translated by R. S. Pine-Coffin. Baltimore: Penguin.

Bizjak, Jurij. 1991. *A Key to Job: Translation, Interpretation and Structure of the book of Job*. Jerusalem: Tantur.

Burrell, David. 1963. *Analogy and Philosophical Language*. New Haven, CT: Yale University Press.

———. 1984. "Maimonides, Aquinas and Gersonides on Providence and Evil." *Religious Studies* 20 (1984): 335–51.

———. 1987. *Knowing the Unknowable God: Ibn-Sina, Maimonides, Aquinas*. Notre Dame, IN: University of Notre Dame Press.

———. 1992. "Why Not Pursue the Metaphor of Artisan and View God's Knowledge as Practical?" In *Neoplatonism and Jewish Thought*, edited by Lenn E. Goodman. Albany: State University of New York Press. (Reprinted in Burrell 2004b, ch. 3.)

———. 1993. *Freedom and Creation in Three Traditions*. Notre Dame, IN: University of Notre Dame Press.

———1996. "The Christian Distinction Celebrated and Expanded." In *The Truthful and the Good*, edited by John Drummond and James Hart. Dordrecht: Kluwer Academic Publishers.

———. 2004a. "Theology and Philosophy." In *The Blackwell Companion to Modern Theology*, edited by Gareth Jones. Oxford: Blackwell.

———. 2004b. *Faith and Freedom*. Oxford: Blackwell.

Fingarette, Herbert. 1978. "The Meaning of Law in the Book of Job." *Hastings Law Journal* 29:1581–1617.

Gardet, Louis. 1951. "Les notes d'Avicenne sur *La théologie d'Aristote*." *Révue Thomiste* 51:346–406.

Ghazali, Abu Muhhamad. 1992. *Al-Ghazali on the Ninety-Nine Beautiful Names of God*. Translated by David Burrell and Nazih Daher. Cambridge: Islamic Texts Society.

Goodman, Lenn, trans. 1988. *The Book of Theodicy: Translation and Commentary of the Book of Job*, by Sa'adiah ben Joseph al-Fayyumi. New Haven, CT: Yale University Press.

Goris, Harm. 1996. *Free Creatures of an Eternal God*. Leuven: Peeters.

Grant, Sara. 2002. *Towards an Alternative Theology: Confessions of a Nondualist Christian*. Edited by Bradley Malkovsky. Notre Dame, IN: University of Notre Dame Press.

Guillaume, Alfred, ed. and trans. 1955. *The Life of Muhammad: A Translation of Ichaq's Sirat Rasul Allah*. London: Oxford University Press.

Gutiérrez, Gustavo. 1987. *On Job: God-Talk and the Suffering of the Innocent*. Translated by Mathew J. O'Connell. Maryknoll, NY: Orbis.

Habel, Norman. 1985. *Book of Job: A Commentary*. Philadelphia: Westminster.

Hasker, William. 1989. *God, Time, and Knowledge*. Ithaca, NY: Cornell University Press.

Ibn 'Arabi. 1980. *Fusus al-Hikam*. In R. W. J. Austin, trans., *Ibn al'Arabi The Bezels of Wisdom*. Mahwah, NJ: Paulist Press.

Johns, A. H. 1989. "David and Bathsheba: A Case Study in the Exegesis of Qur'anic Story-telling," *MIDEO 19* [=*Mélanges de l'Institut domnicain dÉtudes Orientales* (Cairo)] 19:225–66.

———. 1999. "Narrative, Intertext and Allusion in the Qur'anic Presentation of Job," *Journal of Qur'anic Studies* 1 (1999):1–25, by permission of the author.

Levi ben Gershom. 1946. *The Commentary of Levi ben Gerson (Gersonides) on the Book of Job*. Translated by A. L. Lassen. New York: Bloch.

Levi ben Gershom. 1977. *Gersonides' The wars of the Lord, Treatise Three: On God's Knowledge*. Translated by Norbert Max Samuelson.

Madkour, Ibrahim. 1934. *La Place d'al-Farabi dans l'école philosophique musulmane*. Paris: Librairie d'Amérique et d'Ouest.

Maimon, Moses. 1956. *The Guide for the Perplexed* Translated by Josef Fried-lander. New York: Dover. (I shall employ the Friedlander translation of Maimonides, unless the more recent and literal rendering of Schlomo Pines [Chicago: University of Chicago, 1963] is indicated.)

Pickstock, Catherine. 1998. *After Writing: On the Liturgical Consummation of Philosophy.* Oxford: Blackwell.

Pieper, Josef. 1967. "The Negative Element in the Philosophy of St. Thomas." In *Silence of St. Thomas.* New York: Pantheon.

Samuelson, Norbert. 1972. "Gersonides' Account of God's Knowledge of Particulars," *Journal of the History of Philosophy* 10, 399–416.

———. 1976. "The Problem of Future Contingents in Medieval Jewish Phi-losophy." *Studies in Medieval Culture* 6/7: 71–82.

———, ed. 1977. *Gersonides on God's Knowledge (Wars of the Lord* III). Toronto: Pontifical Institute of Medieval Studies.

Schimmel, Annemarie. 1975. *Mystical Dimensions of Islam.* Chapel Hill: University of North Carolina Press.

Sherry, Patrick. 1984. *Spirit, Saints, and Immortality.* London: Macmillan.

Shortt, Rupert. 2005. "Belief and Theology: Some Core Questions." In *God's Advocates: Christian Thinkers in Conversation.* London: Darton Longman and Todd.

Smith, Margaret. 1994. *Rabi'a: The Life and Work of Rabi'a and Other Women Mystics in Islam.* Oxford: One World.

Sokolowski, Robert. 1995. *God of Faith and Reason.* Washington, DC: Catholic University of America Press.

Tilley, Terrence W. 1991. *The Evils of Theodicy.* Washington, DC: Georgetown University Press.

Touati, Charles, trans. 1968. *Les Guerres du Seigneur, Livres III et IV,* by Levi ben Gerson. Le Haye: Mouton.

Weinandy, Thomas. 1985. *Does God Change?: The Word's Becoming in the Incarnation.* Still River, MA: St. Bede's Publications.

Wilcox, John T. 1989. *The Bitterness of Job: A Philosophical Reading.* Ann Arbor: University of Michigan Press.

Williams, Rowan. 1991. *Teresa of Avila.* London: Geoffrey Chapman.

Wittgenstein, Ludwig. 1961. *Tractatus logico-philosophicus.* London: Routledge and Kegan Paul.

———. 1967. *Zettel.* Oxford: Basil Blackwell.

Zuckerman, Bruce. 1991. *Job the Silent: A Study in Historical Counterpoint.* New York: Oxford University Press.

# INDEX